AF350853

TEST PREP MATH BOOK
FOR CASAS MATH GOALS 2 LEVEL D

Helping Learners Approach Math with Confidence while Preparing them for CASAS Math GOALS 2 Level D—**Forms 927M and 928M**

By

Copyright ©2024 Coaching for Better Learning, LLC

All rights reserved.

TABLE OF CONTENT

PREFACE

Dear Instructors,

This Test Prep math book is specifically designed to prepare adult learners for the CASAS Math GOALS 2 Level D Forms 927M and 928M. It fully aligns with the CASAS Competencies and meets the requirements of the College and Career Reading Standards (CCRS), the National Reporting System (NRS), and the Workforce Innovation and Opportunity Act (WIOA).

Adhering to the CASAS test blueprint, this textbook covers mathematical areas through six detailed chapters: *Number Sense and Operations; Consumer Economics; Algebraic Thinking; Geometry; Data Analysis, Statistics and Probability and Pure Mathematics.*

The book's content is structured to improve the mathematical thinking skills of adult students. It provides 14 lessons across various competencies, such as Consumer Economics, Community Resources, Employment, and Pure Mathematics. Each chapter is thoughtfully crafted with multiple lessons to foster deep understanding and practical application of mathematical concepts.

Additionally, the book includes two practice tests that simulate the actual CASAS assessments, incorporating real-world math problems to give students a genuine taste of what they can expect. Complete with answer keys for all exercises and practice tests, this textbook is a robust tool for effective learning and assessment.

Using this resource in your teaching will equip you to effectively develop and improve the math strategies, functions, and concepts necessary for your adult learners' success. Indeed, this book is an invaluable asset for programs that aim to empower their students with the mathematical skills required for success in everyday contexts such as community involvement, family management, and professional environments. To order class sets, go to cbledu.com.

INTRODUCTION

Dear Math Students,

Welcome to your journey toward improving your math skills with this test-prep math textbook. It is designed specifically for adult learners like you. This book is structured to prepare you for the CASAS Math GOALS 2 Level D test. In the six chapters, you'll explore essential mathematical areas, including *Number Sense and Operations; Consumer Economics; Algebraic Thinking; Geometry; Data Analysis, Statistics and Probability and Pure Mathematics*. With 14 practical lessons, this textbook offers a clear path to improving your mathematical knowledge.

Practicing the exercises in this book is crucial. Each chapter includes multiple lessons that build on each other to help you understand and apply mathematical concepts in real-world situations. By engaging with these exercises, you'll develop a stronger foundation in each topic, making sure that you're well-prepared not just for the tests but also for the practical application of these skills in daily life.

We've also included two practice tests that mimic the actual CASAS level D test. These practice tests are designed to give you a realistic experience of what to expect on the actual test. By taking these practice tests, you can assess your progress, identify areas where you need further practice, and build your confidence.

This textbook is more than just a study guide—it's a tool that will equip you with the math strategies, functions, and concepts necessary to solve word problems confidently. Regular practice and study will transform your understanding of math, turning challenges into opportunities for growth and learning.

Remember, math skills are essential for success in various aspects of your life, including community involvement, managing family finances, and professional advancement. By committing to completing the exercises and fully engaging with the materials in this book, you'll be setting yourself up for success in your academic pursuits and beyond.

Let's get started on this path together!

HOW TO APPROACH MATH

Here are ten practical ways you can overcome math fear and anxiety and build confidence while using this math textbook:

1. **Start Small:** Begin with easier problems that you can solve to build your confidence before solving harder ones.

2. **Practice Regularly:** Consistent practice makes math feel more manageable. Try to work on math problems a few times a week.

3. **Use the Book's Resources:** Take advantage of the tools and explanations in your textbook. They are designed to help you understand and solve math problems.

4. **Take Breaks:** If you feel overwhelmed, take a short break. Come back to the problem with a clear mind.

5. **Ask for Help:** Don't hesitate to seek help when you need it. Ask a teacher or a classmate, or use online resources if you're stuck.

6. **Stay Positive:** Keep a positive attitude about math. Remind yourself that you can handle it and that it's okay to make mistakes as you learn.

7. **Set Small Goals:** Break your math studies into small, achievable goals. Celebrate when you reach these goals to motivate yourself.

8. **Understand, Don't Memorize:** Focus on understanding the math concepts rather than just memorizing formulas. This understanding will make you feel more confident in your ability to solve math problems.

9. **Visualize Success:** Picture yourself successfully solving problems and understanding concepts. This visualization can boost your confidence.

10. **Reflect on Progress:** Regularly look back at where you started and recognize the progress you've made. This can be a great confidence booster.

By following these strategies, you'll be better positioned to tackle math with less anxiety and more confidence.

STUDY STRATEGIES

Here are ten simple strategies to study and improve your math knowledge, skills, and understanding using this textbook. Each strategy is designed to be practical and straightforward.

Strategy	Description
1. Set a study schedule.	Allocate specific times each week for math study and practice to build a routine.
2. Create a study space.	Find a quiet, organized space dedicated to studying to stay focused.
3. Use the textbook.	Read explanations and solve problems in the textbook to understand concepts deeply.
4. Practice with examples.	Work through example problems to understand how to apply math rules before trying exercises on your own.
5. Summarize each lesson.	Write a brief summary of what you learned in each lesson to reinforce your understanding.
6. Solve practice tests.	Use practice tests in the textbook to prepare for the actual test and build confidence.
7. Discuss with peers.	Study in groups or discuss problems with classmates to get different perspectives and solutions.
8. Teach someone else.	Explain math concepts to someone else to improve your own understanding and retention.
9. Use online resources.	Supplement your textbook with online tutorials and exercises (e.g., YouTube videos) for additional practice.
10. Review regularly.	Regularly go back and review previous chapters to keep information fresh and build connections between topics and chapters.

Using these strategies can help you make the most of your math textbook and your study time to build up your mathematical abilities and confidence.

CHAPTER 1:
NUMBER SENSE AND OPERATIONS

Lesson 1: Solve real-world mathematical problems involving the four operations and rational numbers.

A rational number is a number that can be written as a **ratio**. In other words, a rational number can be written as a **fraction** in which the numerator and the denominator are whole numbers. Positive and negative numbers, fractions, and decimals are all rational numbers.

Rational Numbers

$$1.086, \quad -50, \quad \frac{2}{7}, \quad 15,239$$

We can solve problems that require using the four operations with rational numbers.

Example 1:

Jerry bought a piece of wood 5.2 meters long. He cut off 5/4 meters from the end. How long is a piece of wood now?

Solution:

Notice that this is a subtraction problem. First, convert 5/4 to decimal. Divide 5 by 4:

$$\frac{5}{4} = 1.25$$

Now, subtract the decimals numbers:

$$5.2 - 1.25 = 3.95$$

Then, the remaining piece of wood is **3.95 meters.**

Example 2:

Tanesha is filling her new fish aquarium. The aquarium holds 50 gallons of water. If she fills the aquarium 3/5 of the way full, how many gallons will she need?

Solution:

First, we multiply 50 by 3/5. Write the whole number as a fraction with a denominator of 1.

$$\frac{50}{1} \times \frac{3}{5}$$

Multiply the numerators and the denominators, and simplify:

$$\frac{50}{1} \times \frac{3}{5} = \frac{150}{5} = 30$$

Then, Tanesha need **30 gallons.**

Practice Exercises

1. Sheryl studied 10.5 hours last month. This month, she studied 9/4 hours less. How long did she study this month? Write your answer in decimal form.

   A. 7.50 hours

   B. 8.75 hours

   C. 12.75 hours

   D. 8.25 hours

2. The selling price of an item is 1.45 times the price the store paid. If the selling price is $145, what did the store pay?

   A. $100.00

   B. $210.22

   C. $143.55

   D. $90.99

> Mike purchased nine smartphones at $345.95 each, plus $15 sales tax. He paid 1/5 of the total with a gift card and put the rest on a company credit card.

3. What is the total cost for nine smartphones?

   A. $3,113.55

   B. $3,200.90

   C. $3,128.55

   D. $3,130.05

4. How much was charged to the credit card?

   A. $625.71

   B. $2,420.84

   C. $2,502.84

   D. $1,256.75

5. Suppose that Mike paid 3/4 of the total with a gift card and put the rest on a company credit card. How much was charged to the credit card? (Round your answer to the nearest cent.)

   A. $2,346.45

   B. $782.14

   C. $2,500.95

   D. $810.55

6. A dog eats 1.85 pounds of food each day. How much food will the dog eat in six weeks?

   A. 77.70 pounds

   B. 11.10 pounds

   C. 12.95 pounds

   D. 34.50 pounds

7. Sarah got a plant as a gift. Her plant grows an average of 0.82 inches every week. How many days does it take for the plant to grow 12.30 inches?

   A. 15 days

   B. 45 days

   C. 90 days

   D. 105 days

8. After spending $18,540 for a car and $3,795 for a motorcycle, Joe had $10,165 left in his bank account. How much money did he have at first?

   A. $32,000

   B. $32,500

   C. $29,700

   D. $22,335

9. The capacity of a pool is 14,850 gallons of water. If the pool is filled to 2/5 of its capacity, how many gallons will be required to fill it?

   A. 5,940 gal

   B. 6,500 gal.

   C. 7,200 gal.

   D. 8,910 gal.

10. Town A has a population of 56,348 people. Town B has 7,590 more people than Town A. The population of Town C is 2.5 times the population of Town B. How many people live in Town C?

   A. 159,845 people

   B. 127,876 people

   C. 161,745 people

   D. 75,523 people

Answer Key:

1)	D	6)	A
2)	A	7)	D
3)	C	8)	B
4)	C	9)	A
5)	B	10)	A

Lesson 2: Understand ratio, rate and percent concepts.

A **ratio** is the comparison of two or more numbers of the same kind. We use ratios to compare things of the same type. There are different ways we can write ratios, and they all mean the same thing:

3 is to 8

3:8

3/8

A **rate** is the ratio (fraction) of two different quantities. A **unit rate** is a rate where the second quantity is one unit, such as $12 per person or 50 miles per hour. "Per person" and "per hour" are the second quantities in each ratio.

Percent means "out of 100." We use the percent symbol (%) as a way to write a fraction with a common denominator of 100. When we write 60%, this is equivalent to the fraction 60/100 or the decimal 0.60. Similarly, 120 out of 200 and 30 out of 50 are also 60%, since:

$$\frac{120}{200} = \frac{30}{50} = \frac{60}{100}$$

Example 1:

Taylor's car can drive 400 miles on a tank of 25 gallons. Find the unit rate of miles per gallon.

Solution:

Divide 400 miles by 25 gallons to find the unit rate.

$$\frac{400 \text{ miles}}{25 \text{ gallons}} = 16 \frac{miles}{gallon}$$

The unit rate is **16 miles per gallon.**

Example 2:

An item originally cost $490. If the price of the item decreases by 8%, what is the new price?

Solution:

Step 1: First, convert 8% to a fraction

$$8\% = \frac{8}{100}$$

Step 2: Simplify the fraction.

$$\frac{8}{100} = \frac{4}{50} = \frac{2}{25}$$

Step 3: Multiply $\frac{2}{25}$ by 490.

$$\frac{2}{25} \times 490 = \frac{980}{25} = 39.2$$

So the decrease in the price of the item is $39.20. Thus, the new price is $490 − $39.20 = **$450.80**

Practice Exercises

1. Which of the following is a unit rate?

    A. 5 pounds/3 weeks

    B. 174 cars per day

    C. 15.5%

    D. 32 out of 100

2. 45 people out of 360 state that they like cats. What percent is this?

    A. 25%

    B. 8%

    C. 15%

    D. 12.5%

> On a farm with 85 animals, there are 35 chickens, 17 pigs, and 33 cows.

3. What is the ratio of the number of pigs to the number of chickens?

    A. 17/35

    B. 35/17

    C. 35/85

    D. 17/85

4. What is the ratio of the number of pigs to all the animals on the farm?

    A. 85/17

    B. 1/7

    C. 33/85

    D. 1/5

5. What is the ratio of the number of chickens to all the animals on the farm?

    A. 1/17

    B. 17/7

    C. 7/17

    D. 7/5

6. The sales tax in a city is 5.7%. How much tax will you pay on a $500 purchase?

    A. $2.80

    B. $280

    C. $25.80

    D. $28.50

7. In the newspaper, James reads that "tuition is expected to increase by 6% next year". If tuition this year was $1,450 per quarter, what would it be next year?

A. $2,320

B. $1,537

C. $1,550

D. $1,600

8. The population of a town increased from 34,650 in 2023 to 36,036 in 2024. What is the percent increase?

A. 5%

B. 10%

C. 40%

D. 4%

9. Which of the following is true?

A. 9 adults per day is a ratio.

B. 1% of 1 is 0.01.

C. 50% of 50 is 5.

D. 200% of 100 is 120.

10. An average person blinks 56 times every 3.5 minutes. How many blinks occur in one minute?

A. 16 blinks per minute

B. 18 blinks per minute

C. 12 blinks per minute

D. 15 blinks per minute

Answer Key:

1) B		6) D	
2) D		7) B	
3) A		8) D	
4) D		9) B	
5) C		10) A	

Lesson 3: Understand the properties of integer exponents, square roots and cube roots.

The **exponent** of a number says **how many times** to use the number in a multiplication.

$$\text{Base} \Rightarrow 2^3 = 2 \times 2 \times 2 = 8 \quad \Leftarrow \text{Exponent}$$

Exponents are also called **powers** or **indices**.

Properties of Integer Exponents

<u>Multiplication of powers with the same base</u>: When we multiply powers with the same base, we **add** the exponents and keep the base.

$$a^m \cdot a^n = a^{m+n}$$

<u>Division of powers with the same base</u>: When we divide powers with the same base, we **subtract** the exponents and keep the base.

$$\frac{a^m}{a^n} = a^{m-n}$$

<u>Powers to powers</u>: To raise a power to another power, we must **multiply** the exponents and keep the base.

$$(a^m)^n = a^{m \cdot n}$$

<u>Negative exponent</u>: A number with a negative exponent is the reciprocal of that number with a positive exponent.

$$a^{-n} = \frac{1}{a^n}$$

<u>Zero exponent</u>: Any nonzero number raised to the power of 0 is equal to 1.

$$a^0 = 1$$

The **square root** of a number is the number that, when multiplied by itself, gives the original number. For example, the square root of 16 is 4 because 4 x 4= 16.

Note: The square root can be positive or negative, as both 4 and −4 squared yield 16.

$$\sqrt{16} = 4 \quad \Rightarrow \quad 4 \times 4 = 16$$

$$\sqrt{16} = -4 \quad \Rightarrow \quad (-4) \times (-4) = 16$$

Notice that square and square roots are inverse operations of each other.

$$\sqrt{16} = 4 \quad \Rightarrow \quad 4 \times 4 = 4^2 = 16$$

The **cube root** of a number is a value that, when multiplied by itself three times, gives the original number. For example, the cube root of 8 is 2 because the integer 2 when multiplied three times, gives the product 8.

$$\sqrt[3]{8} = 2 \quad \Rightarrow \quad 2 \times 2 \times 2 = 8$$

Example 1:

Simplify the following expression:

$$\frac{3^8 \cdot 3^3}{3^4 \cdot 3^2}$$

Solution:

Step 1: First, apply the multiplication of powers with the same base property:

$$3^8 \cdot 3^3 = 3^{8+3} = 3^{11}$$

$$3^4 \cdot 3^2 = 3^{4+2} = 3^6$$

Then, we get

$$\frac{3^{11}}{3^6}$$

Step 2: Apply the division of powers with the same base property.

$$\frac{3^{11}}{3^6} = 3^{11-6} = 3^5$$

Step 3: Simplify.

$$3^5 = 3 \times 3 \times 3 \times 3 \times 3 = 243$$

Thus, the result is:

$$\frac{3^8 \cdot 3^3}{3^4 \cdot 3^2} = \mathbf{243}$$

Example 2:

Simplify

$$\left(\frac{10^{15}}{10^{11}}\right)^{-2}$$

Solution:

Step 1: First, apply the division of powers with the same base property:

$$\frac{10^{15}}{10^{11}} = 10^{15-11} = 10^4$$

Then, we get:

$$(10^4)^{-2}$$

Step 2: Apply the negative exponent property:

$$(10^4)^{-2} = \frac{1}{(10^4)^2}$$

Step 3: Apply the power to a power property:

$$\frac{1}{(10^4)^2} = \frac{1}{10^{4 \cdot 2}} = \frac{1}{10^8}$$

Then, we get:

$$\left(\frac{10^{15}}{10^{11}}\right)^{-2} = \frac{1}{10^8}$$

Example 3:

$$\text{Find } \sqrt{144}$$

Solution:

We know the following:

$$12^2 = 12 \times 12 = 144$$

$$(-12)^2 = (-12) \times (-12) = 144$$

So, the square root of 144 has two possible values: **12 and −12.**

Practice Exercises

1. Simplify the following expression:

$$\frac{9^{19}}{9^9}$$

   A. 9^{28} C. 9^{10}

   B. 9^{171} D. 9

2. Which of the following is equivalent to the following expression?

$$\frac{7^7 \cdot 7^9 \cdot 7^{11}}{7^{20} \cdot 7^0}$$

   A. 7^7 C. 7^{15}

   B. 7^{10} D. 77

3. Which of the following is true?

   A. $\sqrt{1} = 0.5$ C. $6^{24} - 6^{12} = 6^{12}$

   B. $(9)^0 = -1$ D. $\sqrt[3]{125} = 5$

4. What is the value of k?

$$a^9 \cdot a^{2k} = a^{15}$$

   A. 3 C. 4

   B. 6 D. 12

5. Compute the following:

$$\sqrt{1} + \sqrt{16} + \sqrt{81}$$

   A. 1

   B. 8 D. 49

   C. $\sqrt{98}$ E. 14

6. Which expression is equivalent to $\frac{1}{1000}$?

   A. 10^3 C. 10^{-3}

   B. 3^{10} D. 1000^0

7. Simplify the following expression:

$$\frac{(\sqrt{16})^{16}}{4^{16} \cdot 4^2}$$

A. 1/16

B. 16

C. 4

D. 256

8. A dog weighs 10^2 pounds. The weight of a whale weighs one hundred times the weight of the dog. What is the weight of the whale?

A. 10^4 pounds

B. 10^{200} pounds

C. $1,000^2$ pounds

D. 10^5 pounds

9. Which of the following is **false**?

A. The cubic root of 1 is 1.

B. $2^{-1} = 0.5$

C. The square root of 400 is 200.

D. $\sqrt{256} = 16$

10. Which of the following is equivalent to 25^5?

A. 5^{25}

B. 5^{10}

C. 5^{50}

D. 5^5

Answer Key:

1) C	6) C
2) A	7) A
3) D	8) A
4) A	9) C
5) D	10) B

Answer the following reflection questions and feel free to discuss your responses with your teacher or a classmate.

1- What math ideas and principles did you learn in this chapter?

2- What new math concepts did you learn?

3- What procedures or methods did you practice in this chapter?

4- What aspect of this chapter is still not 100% clear to you?

5- What else do you want your teacher to know?

CHAPTER 2: CONSUMER ECONOMICS

Lesson 1: Use measurement and money.

People use money every day, and being able to count it and work out how much change we should be left with is an important life skill. The currency of the US is the United States Dollar (USD). Its symbol is $. American bills or paper currency comes in seven denominations: $1, $2, $5, $10, $20, $50, and $100.

The most commonly used coins in U.S. money are quarters, dimes, nickels, and pennies.

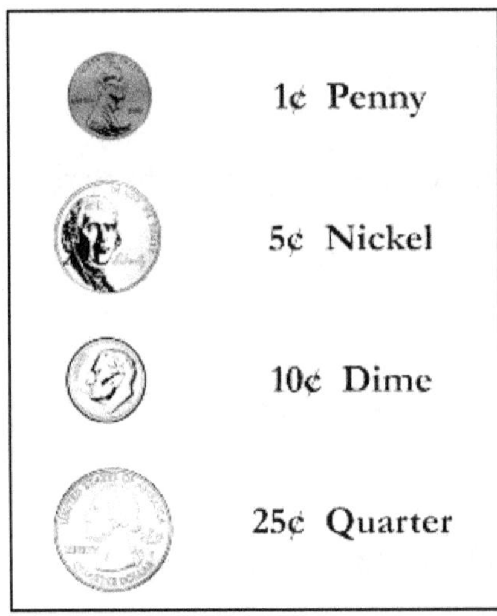

Some Dollar-Related Conversions:

1 dollar = 100 cents, so 1 cent is equal to 0.01 dollars.

1 nickel = 5 cents, so 1 nickel is equal to 0.05 dollars.

1 dime = 10 cents, so 1 dime is equal to 0.1 dollars.

1 quarter = 25 cents, so 1 quarter is equal to 0.25 dollars.

Example 1:

A packet of candy costs 75 cents, and a can of black beans costs $2.65. Kenny buys eight packets of candy and five black bean cans. He pays with a 50-dollar bill. How much change does he get?

Solution:

Step 1: First, convert 75 cents to dollars:

$$75 \text{ cents} = \$0.75$$

Step 2: Calculate the cost of eight packets of candy:

$$8 \times \$0.75 = \$6.00$$

Step 3: Calculate the cost of five cans of black beans:

$$5 \times \$2.65 = \$13.25$$

Step 4: Find the total cost of the items:

$$\$6.00 + \$13.25 = \$19.25$$

Step 5: Subtract $19.25 from $50:

$$\$50 - \$19.25 = \$30.75$$

Thus, Melinda gets **$30.75**

Measurement is a system to measure the length, weight, capacity, time or even amount of certain objects. Here is a list of units of measurement we use to measure different types of quantities:

Length or Height: centimeters, meters, kilometers, feet, yards, miles

Weight: milligrams, grams, kilograms, ounces, pounds, tons

Volume: milliliters, liters, quarts, gallons

Time: seconds, minutes, hours, days, weeks, months, years

Money: dollars, euros, pesos, yen etc.

Temperature: degrees Celsius, degrees Fahrenheit

Example 2:

How many liters are in 7,200 milliliters?

Solution:

We know that 1 liter = 1,000 milliliters. To convert smaller units (milliliters) to larger units (liters), we **divide** the number of smaller units by 1,000.

$$7{,}200 \text{ ml} = 7{,}200 \div 1{,}000 = \textbf{7.2 liters}$$

Practice Exercises

> Rose buys ten pens at 64 cents each, six folders at $1.25 each, and a pencil case at $1.99.

1. What is the total cost?

   A. $14.89   C. $13.99

   B. $15.89   D. $16.50

2. What is the cost of a dozen pens?

   A. $7.68   C. 708 cents

   B. $5.98   D. 668 cents

3. What is the cost of twenty pencil cases?

   A. $40.00   C. $38.70

   B. $39.90   D. $39.80

4. If Rose pays with a 50-dollar bill, how much change does she get?

   A. $44.11   C. $34.11

   B. $35.12   D. $34.21

5. Which of the following is the correct measuring unit for the weight of a bulldozer?

   A. Milligrams   C. Pounds

   B. Ounces   D. Feet

6. Which of the following is the correct measuring unit to measure the capacity of a kitchen sink?

A. Quarts

B. Milliliters

C. Gallons

D. Liters

7. Calvin has seven 10-dollar bills, 15 quarters, and 28 dimes. How much money does he have?

A. $76.55

B. $77.50

C. $78.50

D. $75.65

8. Which of the following is true?

A. 5,000 quarters = $1,200

B. 90 dimes = $9

C. 2 kilometers = 200 meters

D. 1 yard is less than 2.5 feet

9. A baby hippo weighs 250 pounds. The weight of its mom is 12 times as much. What is the weight of its mom in tons? (Hint: 1 ton = 2,000 pounds)

A. 3 tons

B. 2.50 tons

C. 2 tons

D. 1.50 tons

10. Cindy claims there are X quarters in $1,500. What is X?

A. 3,000

B. 4,500

C. 6,000

D. 5,500

Answer Key:

1) B	6) D
2) A	7) A
3) D	8) B
4) C	9) D
5) C	10) C

Lesson 2: Use information to identify and purchase goods and services.

A good is a physical item that can be bought, touched, and used. A service is an action done for people who pay for it.

GOODS AND SERVICES

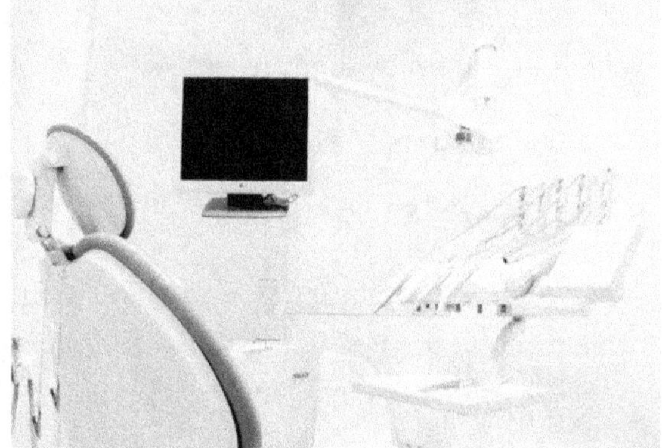

To obtain the best buy, we compare the cost of two or more items and then decide which offers the best value.

To do this, divide the cost by the weight or quantity of the item. Then, we can compare the two items. In other words, to compare prices, we compare the **unit rates** of the items.

Example 1:

At Lou's Grocery, Murray can buy six bags of cookies for $25. At an online shop, the price of nine bags of cookies is $36. Which is the better deal?

Solution:

Find the unit price for each store:

Lou´s Grocery:

$$unit\ rate = \frac{\$25}{6} = \$4.17\ per\ bag$$

Online Store:

$$unit\ rate = \frac{\$36}{9} = \$4\ per\ bag$$

Then, the better deal is 9 bags of cookies for $36 **(lower unit rate).**

Reading bills and receipts is a life skill because almost every household receives at least one type of bill or receipt each month. Understanding how to read bills and receipts can help us budget our money.

Example 2:

According to the following receipt, what is the total cost?

```
            WALL-MART-SUPERSTORE

                    (888) 888 - 8888
                   MANAGER TOD LINGA
                   888 WALL STORE ST
                 WALL ST CITY, LA 88888

ST# 2323 OP#        23432435 TE#      51      TR#  4354
HAND TOWEL          075953630184                2.97 X
GATORADE            068949055223                2.00 X
T-SHIRT             036231552452               16.88 X
PUSH PINS           088348997350                1.24 X

                          SUBTOTAL             23.09
                TAX 1        7.89%              2.90
                TAX 2        4.90%              1.28
                             TOTAL               ?
                     CREDIT  TEND
                     CHANGE  DUE               0.00
```

Solution:

To find the total amount, add subtotal, tax 1 and tax 2:

Total amount = $23.09 + $2.90 + $1.28 = **$27.27**

Look at the following receipt:

The Lone Pine
43 Manchester Road
12480 Brisbane
Australia
617-3236-6207

```
Invoice 08000008                    09/04/08
Table    25                           12:45

   2 Carlsberg Bottle                  16.00
   3 Heineken Draft Standard           24.60
   1 Heineken Draft Half Liter         15.20
   2 Carlsberg Bucket (5 bottles)      80.00
   4 Grilled Chicken Breast            74.00
   3 Sirloin Steak                     96.00
   1 Coke                               3.50
   5 Ice Cream                         18.00
   ─────────────────────────────────────────
      Subtotal                        327.30
      Sales/Gov Tax - 5%                  ?
      Service Charge - 10%             32.73
   ─────────────────────────────────────────
      GRAND TOTAL                         ?

Thank you and          Cash           400.00
see you again!         Change             ?
```

1. How many items were purchased?

    A. 8

    B. 11

    C. 20

    D. 21

2. Which item is the cheapest?

    A. Ice cream

    B. Sirloin steak

    C. Carlsberg bottle

    D. Coke

3. What is the sales/gov tax?

    A. $16.37

    B. $32.73

    C. $15.35

    D. $16.45

4. What is the total amount?

    A. $400.00

    B. $376.40

    C. $360.03

    D. $375.85

5. What is the change?

    A. $39.97

    B. $25.15

    C. $23.60

    D. $26.38

6. What is the cost of nine ice creams?

    A. $162.00

    B. $34.56

    C. $32.40

    D. $35.00

Look at the following table:

Gas Station	Number of gallons	Cost
1	45	$134.55
2	30	$92.70
3	40	$124.40

7. What is the unit price for Gas Station 2 in dollars per gallon?

A. $3.09 per gallon

B. $3.10 per gallon

C. $3.59 per gallon

D. $3.19 per gallon

8. What is the best deal?

A. Gas Station 2

B. Gas Station 1

C. Gas Station 3

9. What is the cost of 60 gallons of gas at Gas Station 3?

A. $186.00

B. $186.60

C. $185.50

D. $185.40

10. If Tamika has $60 to spend on gas, what is the maximum number of gallons she can buy at Gas Station 1?

A. 16 gallons

B. 18 gallons

C. 20 gallons

D. 21 gallons

Answer Key:

1) D	6) C
2) D	7) A
3) A	8) B
4) B	9) B
5) C	10) C

REFLECTION ON LEARNING

Answer the following reflection questions and feel free to discuss your responses with your teacher or a classmate.

1- What math ideas and principles did you learn in this chapter?

2- What new math concepts did you learn?

3- What procedures or methods did you practice in this chapter?

4- What aspect of this chapter is still not 100% clear to you?

5- What else do you want your teacher to know?

(decorative chalkboard equations background)

CHAPTER 3:
ALGEBRAIC THINKING

Lesson 1: Solve problems involving proportional relationships, linear equations and pairs of simultaneous linear equations.

Proportional relationships are relationships between two variables when **their ratios are equivalent.** An equation of two equivalent ratios is called **a proportion**.

An equation is said to be **linear** when all the variables have the highest power equal to one.

Linear equation

$$2x - 5 = 16$$

Simultaneous linear equations are two or more algebraic equations that share variables such as x and y. They are called simultaneous equations because the equations are solved at the same time.

$$7x - 9y = -8$$

$$3x + 7y = 12$$

<u>**Example 1:**</u>

A 5-pound bag of potatoes costs \$2.79. How much does 24 pounds of potatoes cost?

Solution:

We can set up the following proportion that represents the problem:

$$\frac{5\ pounds}{\$2.79} = \frac{24\ pounds}{x}$$

Solve for x:

$$\frac{5\ pounds}{\$2.79} = \frac{24\ pounds}{x}$$

$$(5\ pounds) \cdot x = (24\ pounds) \cdot \$2.79$$

$$x = \frac{(24 \; pounds) \cdot \$2.79}{5 \; pounds} = \$13.39$$

Then, 24 pounds of potatoes cost **$13.39.**

Example 2:

A farmer cuts a 360-foot fence into two pieces of different sizes. The longer piece should be three times as long as the shorter piece. How long are the two pieces?

Solution:

Let x be the length of the shorter piece. Set up the equation that represents the problem:

$$x + 3x = 360$$

Solve the equation by combining like terms:

$$\mathbf{x + 3x} = 360$$

$$\mathbf{4x} = 360$$

We want to remove 4 in the equation. To remove 4, do the opposite. In this case, divide both sides of the equation by 4 to solve for x.

$$\frac{4x}{4} = \frac{360}{4}$$

$$x = 90$$

Thus, the lengths of the two pieces are:

$$\text{Shorter piece} = \mathbf{90 \; feet}$$

$$\text{Longer piece} = 90 \times 3 = \mathbf{270 \; feet}$$

Example 3:

In a summer festival, 85 tickets were sold. Adult tickets cost $5.00 each, children's tickets cost $2.50 each, and a total of $300 was collected. How many tickets of each kind were sold?

Solution:

Step 1: Define the variables. Let x be the number of adult tickets. Let y be the number of children's tickets. Now, we write two equations that represent the problem:

1) Total number of tickets: $x + y = 85$

2) Total money collected: $5x + 2.5y = 300$

So, we got the simultaneous linear equations that represent the problem:

$$1) \quad x + y = 85$$

$$2) \quad 5x + 2.5y = 300$$

Step 2: Solve the system of linear equations. Isolate y in the first equation:

$$x + y = 85 \quad \Rightarrow \quad y = 85 - x$$

Replace this value of y into the second equation:

$$5x + 2.5(85 - x) = 300$$

Step 3: Solve the equation:

$$5x + 2.5(85 - x) = 300$$

$$5x + 212.5 - 2.5x = 300$$

$$5x - 2.5x = 300 - 212.5$$

$$2.5x = 87.5$$

$$x = \frac{87.5}{2.5} = \mathbf{35}$$

Step 4: Now, put the value of x in the first equation to find y:

$$x + y = 85$$

$$35 + y = 85$$

$$y = 85 - 35 = \mathbf{50}$$

Then, the number of adult tickets is **35** and the number of children's tickets is **50**.

<u>Note</u>: there are several ways to solve a system of linear equations.

Practice Exercises

1. Dave checks his pulse for 2 minutes and counts 168 beats. How many beats are in five minutes?

    A. 840

    B. 420

    C. 560

    D. 336

2. Cellular phone service is available for $72 per month for 1,250 minutes. What is the monthly cost per minute?

   A. $10.05

   B. $0.66

   C. $0.0576

   D. $17.36

> A steel beam 44 inches in length is cut into two smaller beams. One of the new beams is 9 inches longer than the other. Let x be the length of the shorter beam.

3. Which equation represents this situation?

   A. $x + x - 9 = 44$

   B. $2x - 9 = 44$

   C. $x + 9x = 44$

   D. $x + x + 9 = 44$

4. What is the length of the shorter beam?

   A. 18.5 in.

   B. 16 in.

   C. 17.5 in.

   D. 26.7 in.

5. What is the length of the longer beam?

   A. 26.5 in.

   B. 28 in.

   C. 17.5 in.

   D. 29 in.

> A high school is selling tickets to a musical show. On Thursday, the school sold 10 adult tickets and 8 child tickets for a total of $147. On Friday, the school sold 9 adult tickets and 10 child tickets for a total of $150.50. Let x be the cost per adult ticket and y be the cost per child ticket.

6. What is the pair of simultaneous linear equations that represents this situation?

    A. $10x + 8y = 150.50$ and $9x + 10y = 147$

    B. $10x + 8y = 147$ and $9x + 10y = 150.50$

    C. $10x - 8y = 147$ and $9x - 10y = 150.50$

    D. $8x + 10y = 147$ and $10x + 9y = 150.50$

7. What is the cost of one adult ticket?

    A. $9.00

    B. $9.50

    C. $8.50

    D. $6.50

8. What is the cost of one child ticket?

    A. $6.50

    B. $5.75

    C. $9.50

    D. $4.45

9. A vanilla milkshake costs $2.50 less than a fruit smoothie. If 4 vanilla milkshakes and 3 fruit smoothies cost $32, what is the cost of a fruit smoothie?

    A. $4.50

    B. $7.50

    C. $6.00

    D. $3.50

10. Twice a number minus 18 is equal to the number. What is the number?

   A. 36

   B. 24

   C. 18

   D. 20

Answer Key:

1) B		6) B
2) D		7) B
3) D		8) A
4) C		9) C
5) A		10) C

Lesson 2: Use algebraic expressions to solve real-world mathematical problems.

An **algebraic expression** is an expression that can include numbers, fractions, parentheses, operation signs and variables (letters). It represents a value that can be found by substituting numbers for the variables.

> **Algebraic Expressions:**
>
> $$h = 4.5m - 8$$
>
> $$y = 5x + 7$$
>
> $$s = t^2 - 0.5y$$

Algebraic expressions are useful because they represent the value of an expression for all of the values a variable can take on. When we describe an expression in words that includes a variable, we describe an algebraic expression: an expression with a variable.

We can solve word problems using algebraic expressions with letters to represent the problem, simple contextual math situations, or real-world mathematical problems.

Example 1:

Write an algebraic expression for "75% of a number."

Solution:

Let x be the number. To express 75% of x, we convert 75% to its decimal form, which is 0.75. Then, the algebraic expression for 75% of x is the following:

$$75\% \ of \ x = 0.75x$$

Example 2:

Jack sells computer accessories. His income consists of $375 per week plus a commission of 12% of his sales.

a) Write an algebraic expression for Jack's weekly income in terms of his sales.

b) Find Jack's income for a week in which he sells $650 worth of computer accessories.

Solution:

a) Let N be Jack's total income for the week, and let T be the total amount of his sales. We write an algebraic expression that represents this situation:

$$\text{Income} = \$375 + 12\% \text{ of his sales}$$

$$\mathbf{N = 375 + 0.12T}$$

b) Replace $T = 650$ in the previous expression:

$$N = 375 + 0.12(650)$$

$$N = 375 + 78 = 453$$

Then, Jack's income for the week is **$453**

Practice Exercises

1. Which algebraic expression represents this phrase "a number increased by 15%"?

    A. 0.15x

    B. 15x

    C. 1.15x

    D. 1.50x

> A delivery service charges $3.75 per pound to deliver a package from City A to City B. Nancy wants to mail a package that weighs 12.50 pounds plus whatever packing material she uses. Let C be the shipping cost and p be the weight of the packing material.

2. Which expression represents the cost of shipping Nancy's package?

    A. $C = 3.75 \, (12.50) + p$

    B. $C = 3.75p + 12.50$

    C. $C = 3.75 \, (12.50 + p)$

    D. $12.50 \, (3.75 + p)$

3. What is the shipping cost if Nancy uses 3.10 pounds of packing material?

    A. $58.50

    B. $78.50

    C. $85.63

    D. $60.65

4. What is the shipping cost if Nancy does not use packing material?

   A. $16.25

   B. $21.55

   C. $39.25

   D. $46.88

5. Chris wrote the following algebraic expression: $-\frac{x}{2}$. What would be the phrase that represents this expression?

   A. 37 increased by half of a number

   B. 37 decreased by half of a number

   C. Half of a number minus 37

   D. 37 decreased by twice a number

6. Mr. Fisher bought m books for $113.90. Which expression represents the average cost of each book?

   A. 113.90m

   B. $\dfrac{113.90}{m}$

   C. $\dfrac{m}{113.90}$

   D. 113.90 + m

> Warren has sold 16 more than twice the bicycles as John has.
> Let n be the number of bicycles John sold.

7. Which expression represents the number of bicycles Warren sold?

   A. n + 2 + 16

   B. 2n + 16

   C. 2n − 16

   D. $16 + n^2$

8. If John sold nine bicycles, how many bicycles did Warren sell?

   A. 34

   B. 27

C. 32

D. 30

9. If Warren sold 50 bicycles, how many bicycles did John sell?

   A. 19

   B. 25

   C. 23

   D. 17

10. A smartphone costs x dollars and an additional 5.5% sales tax. Which expression represents the total cost of the smartphone?

    A. $x + 0.55x$

    B. $1.5x + x$

    C. $x + 0.055x$

    D. $x - 0.055x$

Answer Key:

1) C		6) B	
2) C		7) B	
3) A		8) A	
4) D		9) D	
5) B		10) C	

Lesson 3: Use linear functions to model relationships between quantities.

Linear functions are algebraic equations whose graphs are **straight lines**. These equations involve variables (like x and y) and constants. Each term is either a constant or the product of a constant, and (the first power of) a single variable.

For example, the equation **y = mx + b** is a linear function.

- x and y are variables.

- m and b are constants.

  m determines the slope of the line, showing how steep it is.

  b is the y-intercept, the point where the line crosses the y-axis.

Note that the exponent of x is one (first power), making it a linear function.

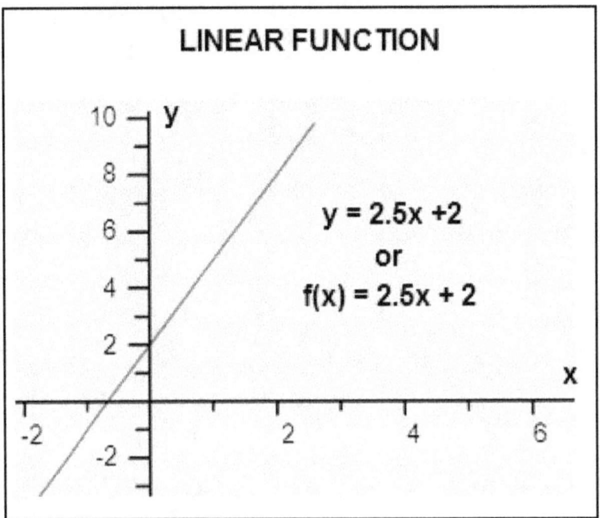

We can model several relationships between quantities as linear functions. Linear relationships are defined by a **straight line** when graphed and allow making an easy prediction based on the consistent rate of change.

Example 1:

A town's population has been growing linearly. In 2020, the population was 15,600. By 2023, the population had grown to 16,800. Suppose that this trend continues.

a) Find the population in 2030.

b) When will the population reach 50,000 people?

Solution:

Notice that the two changing quantities are the population and time. To find the population in 2030, we need **a linear equation** for the population. We got two input-output pairs. The input is *t* years since 2020, and the output is *P(t)*, the town's population.

$$\text{Year 2020: } t = 0, P = 15{,}600 \implies (0, 15, 600)$$

$$\text{Year 2023: } t = 3, P = 16{,}800 \implies (3, 16, 800)$$

Next, we compute the rate of change of the linear model (slope of the linear equation):

$$m = \frac{y_2 - y_1}{x_2 - x_1}$$

In our case, $x_1 = 0$, $y_1 = 15{,}600$, $x_2 = 3$, and $y_2 = 16{,}800$

$$m = \frac{16{,}800 - 15{,}600}{3 - 0} = \frac{1{,}200}{3} = 400$$

Notice that the rate of change is 400 people per year. The y-intercept is the initial population 15, 600 (when t = 0). Therefore, the function that models this problem is:

$$\boldsymbol{P(t) = 400t + 15{,}600}$$

To find the population in 2030, we evaluate the previous function at t = 10. Note that 2030 - 2020 = 10.

$$P(10) = 400(10) + 15{,}600$$

$$P(10) = 4{,}000 + 15{,}600 = 19{,}600$$

So, the population in 2030 will be **19,600 people.**

To find when the population will reach 50,000, we can set P(t) = 50,000 and solve for t.

$$P(t) = 50{,}000$$

$$400t + 15{,}600 = 40{,}000$$

$$400t = 40{,}000 - 15{,}600$$

$$400t = 34{,}400 \implies t = \frac{34{,}400}{400} = 86$$

Then, the population will reach 50,000, 86 years after 2020. In other words, the population will reach 50,000 in 2106.

Example 2:

The following graph shows the speed of a car during a race.

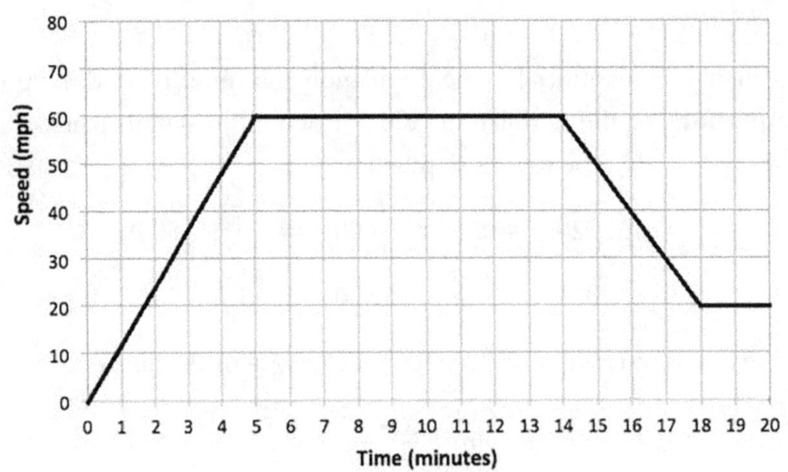

According to the graph, what is likely occurring between the 0-minute and the 5-minute period of the race?

Solution:

During the 0-minute and the 5-minute period of the race, the driver goes from 0 mph, displayed on the y-axis of the graph, to 60 mph. Notice the line between those two points is increasing in a positive direction (positive slope).

Therefore, the car driver is **increasing his speed.**

Practice Exercises

In 2005, the bear population in a park was 458. By 2010, the population was determined to be 563. Suppose that the population continues to change linearly.

1. What is the rate change of this linear model?

   A. 76 bears per year

   B. 21 bears per year

   C. 105 bears per year

   D. 102 bear per year

2. Which linear function represents the bear population P, in terms of t, the years since 2005?

   A. $P(t) = 42t + 458$

   B. $P(t) = 42t + 563$

   C. $P(t) = 21t + 458$

   D. $P(t) = 21t + 563$

3. What is the bear population in 2017?

   A. 815

   B. 962

   C. 770

   D. 710

4. When will the population reach 1,088 bears?

A. Year 2030

C. Year 2028

B. Year 2035

D. Year 2036

The following graph shows the distance two cars have traveled along the freeway over several hours.

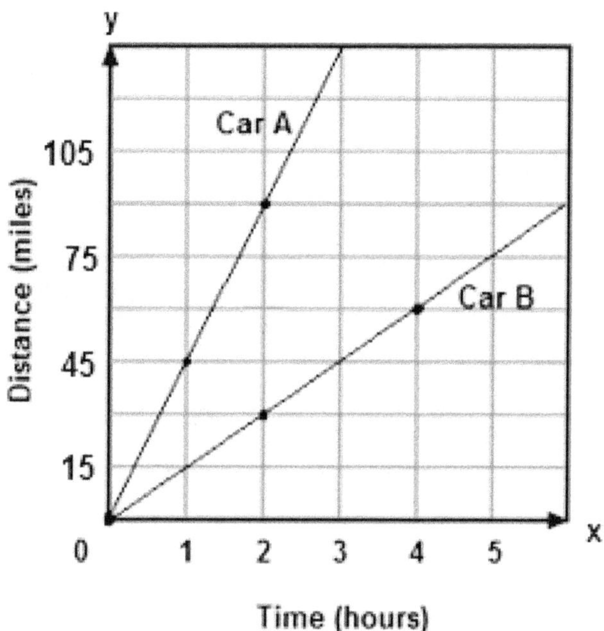

5. What is the slope of the line represented by Car A?

A. 45

C. 35

B. 30

D. 40

6. What is the slope of the line represented by Car B?

A. 15

C. 35

B. 25

D. 30

7. What do the slopes of the lines mean?

A. The time of the travel

C. The speed of the cars

B. The number of hours per mile

D. The total distance traveled by the cars

8. What is the distance traveled by Car A in 5 hours? (Hint: Find the linear function for Car A.)

A. 200 miles

C. 225 miles

B. 215 miles

D. 175 miles

9. What is the distance traveled by Car B in 8 hours? (Hint: Find the linear function for Car B)

    A. 120 miles.   C. 150 miles.

    B. 90 miles.   D. 180 miles.

10. The linear model of a helicopter's descent gives its height a function of time. Which of the following is true?

    A. The initial height is 0.

    B. The rate of change of the model is positive.

    C. The rate of change of the model is negative.

    D. None of the above.

Answer Key:

1) B	6) A
2) C	7) C
3) D	8) C
4) B	9) A
5) A	10) C

REFLECTION ON LEARNING

Answer the following reflection questions and feel free to discuss your responses with your teacher or a classmate.

1- What math ideas and principles did you learn in this chapter?

2- What new math concepts did you learn?

3- What procedures or methods did you practice in this chapter?

4- What aspect of this chapter is still not 100% clear to you?

5- What else do you want your teacher to know?

CHAPTER 4: GEOMETRY

Lesson 1: Compare two-dimensional and three-dimensional shapes.

In geometry, shapes can be classified into two-dimensional (2-D) and three-dimensional (3-D) categories based on their properties.

A **two-dimensional shape** is a flat plane figure or a shape that has two dimensions (length and width). Two-dimensional or 2-D shapes do not have any thickness and can be measured in only two faces.

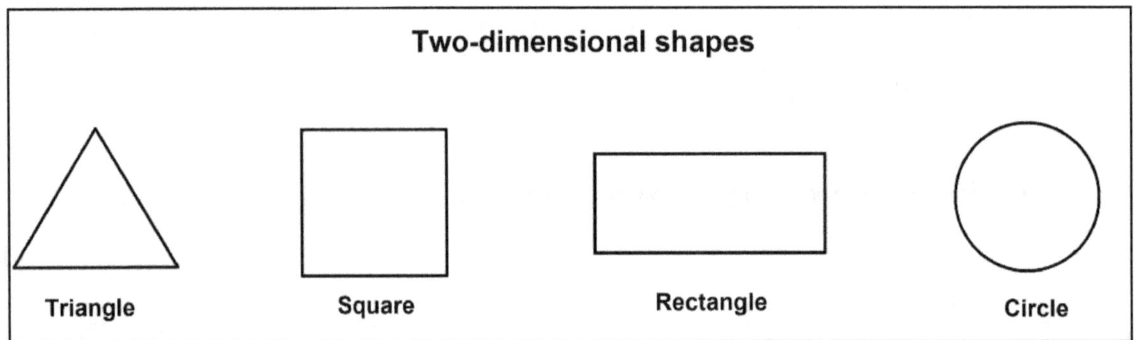

A **three-dimensional shape** is a solid figure or shape that has three dimensions (length, width and height). Three-dimensional shapes have thickness or depth. The attributes of a three-dimensional figure are faces, edges and corners. The three dimensions compose the edges of a 3-D geometric shape.

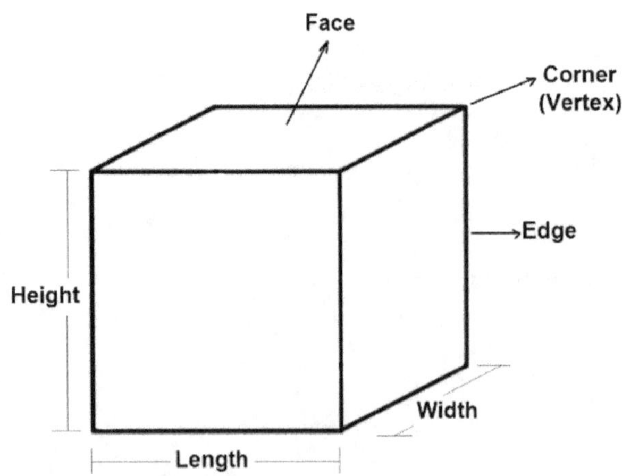

Three-dimensional shapes

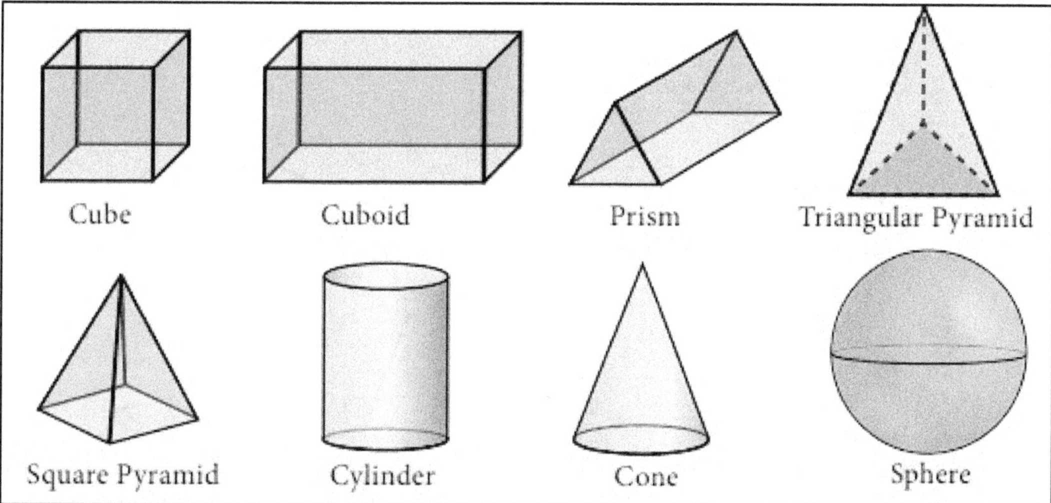

We can analyze and compare two and three-dimensional shapes in different sizes and orientations, using informal language to describe their similarities, differences, and other features.

Example 1:

What is the difference between the following two shapes?

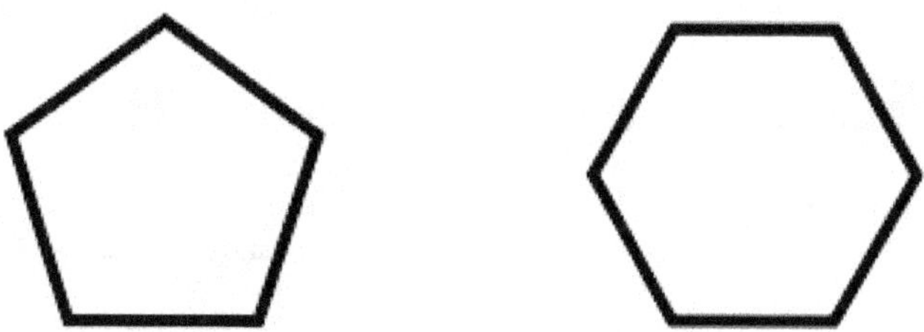

Solution:

Notice that both of these shapes are two-dimensional shapes (pentagon and hexagon), because they are flat.

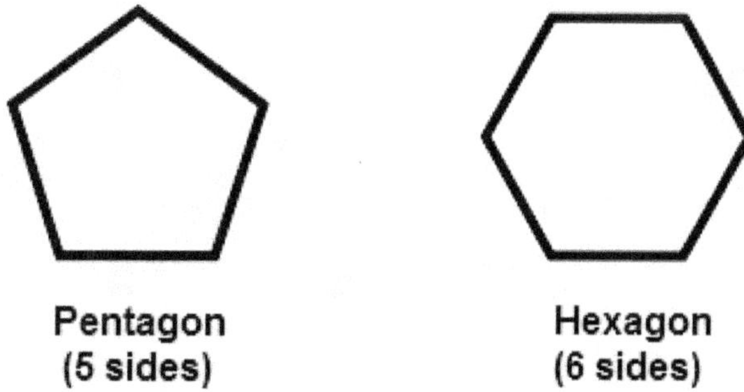

Then, the difference between them is **the number of sides they each have.**

Example 2:

What is similar about the following two shapes?

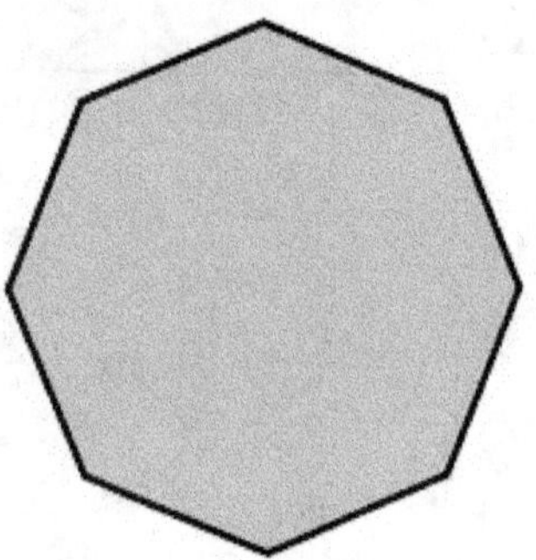
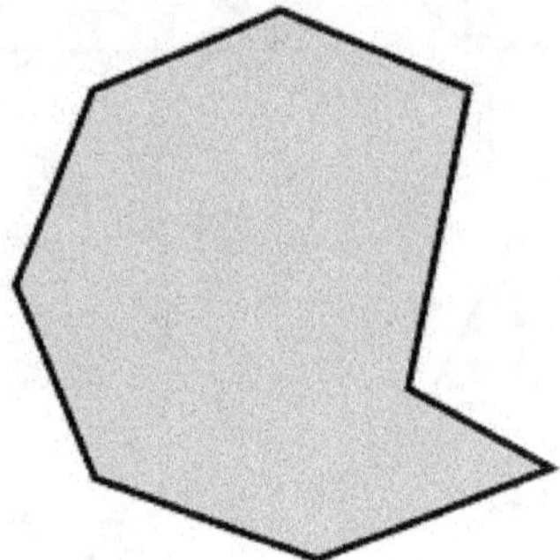

Solution:

Note that both of these shapes are two-dimensional shapes because they are flat. Also, both shapes have **eight sides and eight corners.**

Practice Exercises

1. What is the difference between the following two shapes?

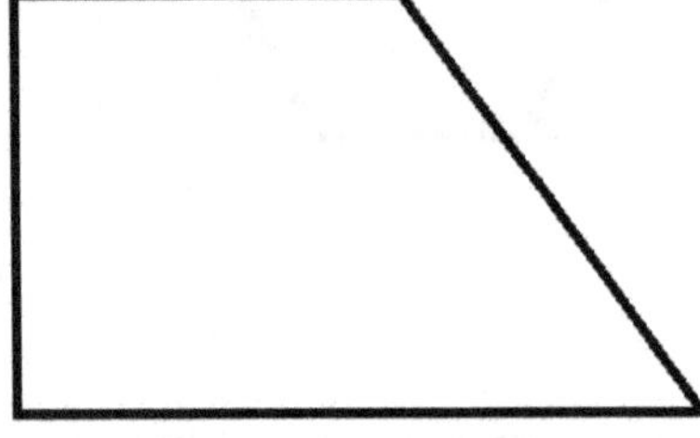
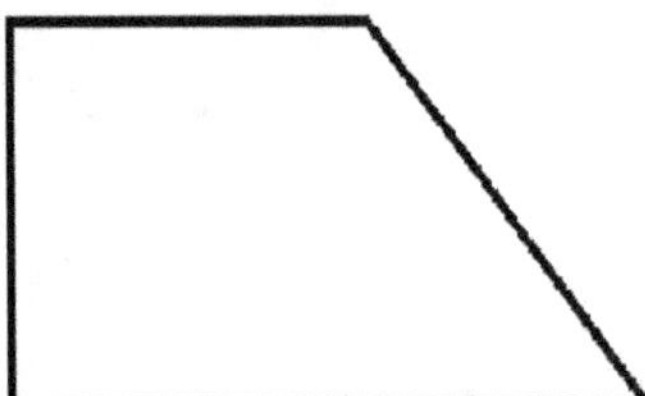

    A. The number of corners

    B. The number of sides

    C. The measure of the angles

    D. Their sizes

2. Which shape has more corners?

    A. Hexagon

    B. Octagon

C. Pentagon

D. Circle

Look at the following shapes

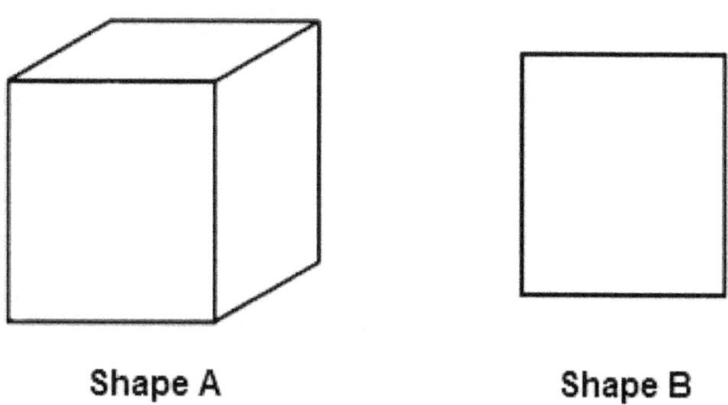

Shape A   Shape B

3. Which of the following is true?

    A. Shape A has seven corners.

    B. Both shapes have the same size.

    C. Both shapes have the same number of sides.

    D. Shape A has six faces.

4. What is the difference between Shape A and Shape B?

    A. Their sizes

    B. The number of sides

    C. Shape A is three-dimensional and Shape B is two-dimensional.

    D. None of the above.

5. What three-dimensional shape has the most corners?

    A. Pentagon

    B. Cylinder

    C. Square pyramid

    D. Cube

6. If a cube has x corners and a triangular pyramid has y faces, what is the value of x + y?

    A. 12

    B. 7

C. 6

D. 10

7. Bruce draws six squares, nine rectangles, and five pentagons. How many sides did Bruce draw?

A. 80

B. 85

C. 84

D. 78

Look at the following shapes:

Shape 1

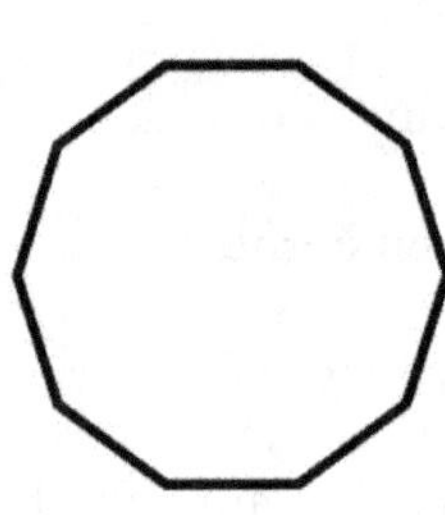

Shape 2

8. How many corners does Shape 1 have?

A. 5

B. 8

C. 10

D. 12

9. Which of the following is true?

A. Both shapes are three-dimensional.

B. Shape 1 has more sides than Shape 2.

C. Both shapes are the same size.

D. Both shapes have the same number of corners.

10. How many edges does a rectangular prism (cuboid) have?

A. 12

B. 10

C. 8

D. 6

Answer Key:

1) D	6) A
2) B	7) B
3) D	8) C
4) C	9) D
5) D	10) A

Lesson 2: Solve real-world problems involving volume and surface area.

The **surface area** of a three-dimensional object is the total area of all its faces. The **volume** is the amount of space occupied by a three-dimensional shape.

Surface Area and Volume of Common Three-Dimensional Shapes

CUBE	CUBOID	CYLINDER
SURFACE AREA TOTAL $A = 6l^2$ SIDES $A = 4l^2$ VOLUME $V = l^3$	SURFACE AREA TOTAL $A = 2(ab + bc + ac)$ SIDES $A = 2(ab + 2ac)$ VOLUME $V = abc$	SURFACE AREA TOTAL $A = 2\pi r(r + h)$ CURVED $A = 2\pi rh$ VOLUME $V = \pi r^2 h$
CONE	SPHERE	HEMISPHERE
SURFACE AREA TOTAL $A = \pi r^2 + \pi rl$ CURVED $A = \pi rl$ VOLUME $V = \frac{1}{3}\pi r^2 h$	SURFACE AREA $A = 4\pi r^2$ VOLUME $V = \frac{4}{3}\pi r^3$	SURFACE AREA TOTAL $A = 3\pi r^2$ CURVED $A = 2\pi r^2$ VOLUME $V = \frac{2}{3}\pi r^3$

Example 1:

Find the surface area and volume of the following three-dimensional shape:

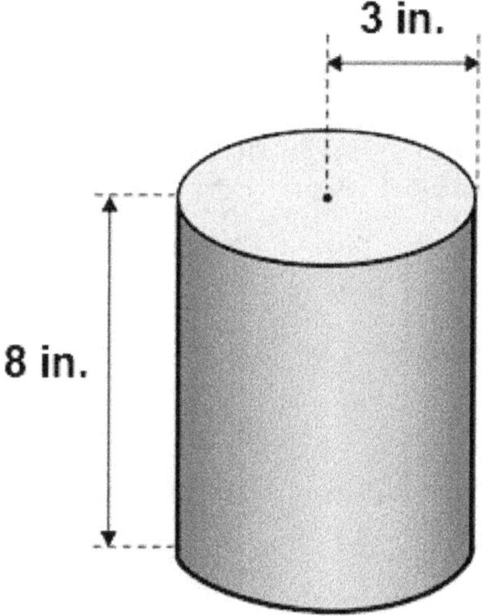

Solution:

Notice that the shape is a cylinder, and the dimensions of the cylinder are as follows: radius = 3 in. and height = 8 in. Apply the formula of the surface area of the cylinder:

$$A = 2\pi r(r + h)$$

$$A = 2 \cdot 3.14 \cdot 3 \; in \, (3 \; in + 8 \; in)$$

$$A = (18.84 \; in)(11 \; in) = \boldsymbol{207.24 \; in^2}$$

Apply the formula of the volume of the cylinder:

$$V = \pi r^2 h$$

$$V = 3.14(3 \; in)^2(8 \; in) = \boldsymbol{226.08 \; in^3}$$

Example 2:

A rectangular fish tank that is 50 inches by 25 inches by 30 inches is 3/5 full of water. Find the volume of water still needed to fill the tank completely.

Solution:

Find the volume of the rectangular fish tank.

Note that the rectangular fish tank is a rectangular prism. The formula for the volume of a rectangular prism is:

Volume = Length x Height x Width

Volume = 50 inches x 25 inches x 30 inches

Volume = 37,500 in^3

Since the rectangular tank is 3/5 full of water, we know we need 2/5 of the volume of the rectangular tank to fill the tank completely with water. Find 2/5 of the volume of the rectangular tank.

$$\frac{2}{5} \times 37,500 \text{ in}^3 = \frac{75,000 \text{ in}^3}{5} = 15,000 \text{ in}^3$$

Then, the volume of water still needed to fill the tank completely is **15,000 in³**

Practice Exercises

The dimensions of a rectangular box are 7.5 in. x 10.5 in. x 6 in.

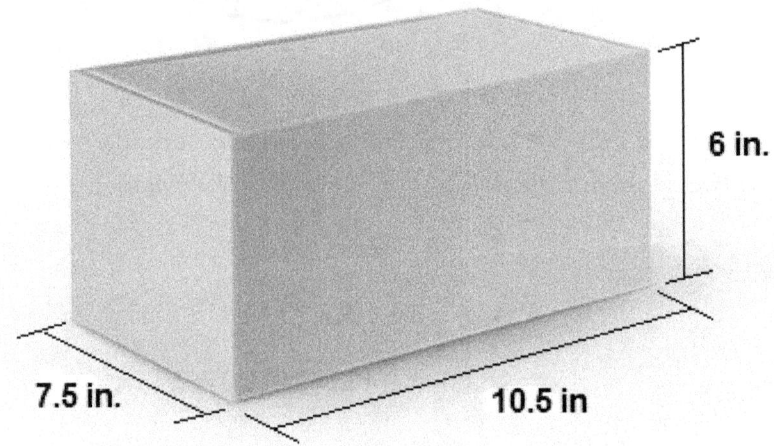

1. What is the total surface area of the box?

   A. 216.7 in²

   B. 373.5 in²

   C. 410.25 in²

   D. 355.5 in²

2. What is the volume of the box?

   A. 472.5 in³

   B. 480 in³

   C. 462.5 in³

   D. 500.2 in³

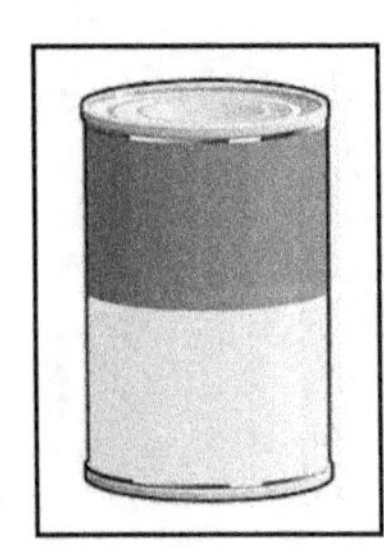

A soup can has a radius of x inches and a height of 6 inches. The volume of the can is 37.5π inches.

3. What is x?

    A. 3 in.   C. 2 in.

    B. 3.5 in.   D. 2.5 in.

4. What is the surface area of the soup can?

    A. 50π in^2 C. 42.5π in^2

    B. 45.5π in^2 D. 39.25π in^2

A farmer is planning to put new material on the conical roof of his silo as shown below:

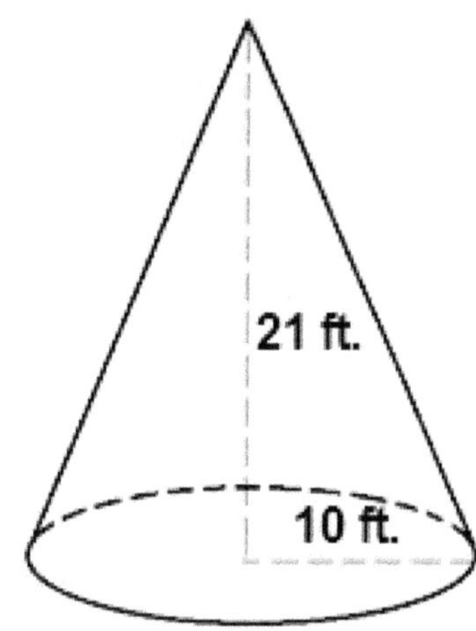

5. What is the number of square feet of roofing material needed? (Use $\pi = 3.14$)

    A. 1,044.35 ft^2 C. 998.73 ft^2

    B. 730.34 ft^2 D. 1,117.32 ft^2

6. What is the volume of the silo? (Use $\pi = 3.14$)

    A. 6,594 ft^3 C. 5,603 ft^3

    B. 3,459.5 ft^3 D. 2,198 ft^3

7. What is the volume of air in a beach ball that has a 15-inch diameter? (Use $\pi = 3.14$)

    A. 1,766.25 in^3 C. 2,826 in^3

    B. 2,461.76 in^3 D. 14,130 in^3

8. If the volume of a cube box is 342 cubic inches, what is the surface area of the cube box?

    A. 294 in^2 C. 147 in^2

    B. 57 in^2 D. 312 in^2

Look at the following can of tomatoes:

9. What is the volume of the can? (Use $\pi = 3.14$)

   A. 188.40 in³

   B. 190.65 in³

   C. 202.34 in³

   D. 197.82 in³

10. How much paper is used for the label on the can of tomatoes?

   A. 131.88 in²

   B. 188.44 in²

   C. 57.20 in²

   D. 147.09 in²

Answer Key:

1) B	6) D
2) A	7) A
3) D	8) A
4) C	9) D
5) B	10) A

Lesson 3: Solve problems with measurement and scale drawings

Scale drawings are drawings that show real objects or figures with proportional dimensions that are reduced or enlarged by a certain amount called **the scale**. These figures are called **similar figures** because their shapes are identical in proportion, although their sizes differ.

In two similar figures, the ratio of their corresponding sides is called the **scale factor**. To find the scale factor, locate two corresponding sides, one on each figure. Then, write the ratio of one side's length to the other side's corresponding length. This shows much one figure has been scaled in comparison to the other.

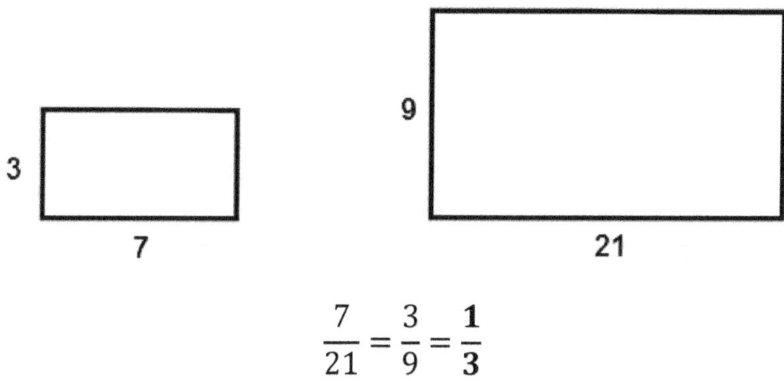

$$\frac{7}{21} = \frac{3}{9} = \frac{1}{3}$$

These two similar rectangles have a scale factor of **1:3** from the small rectangle to the large rectangle. We can interpret and use proportions in solving problems involving dimensions or scale.

Example 1:

A miniature model of a building is made using the scale 3 inches = 7 feet. If the height of the building is 80 feet, what is the height of the miniature model?

Solution:

Let x be the height of the miniature model. Write the proportion that represents the problem.

$$\frac{3 \; inches}{7 \; feet} = \frac{x}{80 \; feet}$$

We have an equation. Solve the equation.

$$\frac{3 \; inches}{7 \; feet} = \frac{x}{80 \; feet}$$

$$(7 \text{ feet}) \cdot x = (3 \text{ inches}) \cdot (80 \text{ feet})$$

$$\Rightarrow \quad x = \frac{(3 \text{ inches}) \cdot (80 \text{ feet})}{7 \text{ feet}} = \frac{240 \text{ inches} \cdot \text{feet}}{7 \text{ feet}} = 34.3 \text{ inches}$$

Then, the height of the miniature model is **34.3 inches.**

Practice Exercises

1. A map of a museum is made using the scale 2.5 inches = 14 feet. If the museum is 15 inches wide in the map, what is the actual width of the museum?

   A. 84 ft.

   B. 90 ft.

   C. 75 ft.

   D. 70 ft.

The following figure is a scaled drawing of a rectangular yard. The scale drawing is 1:25

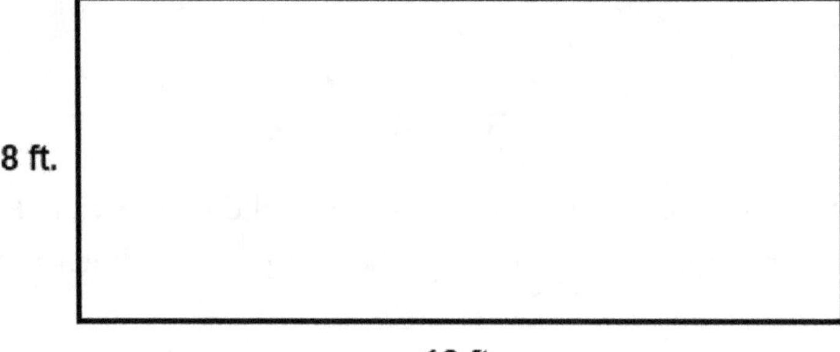

2. What is the actual length of the yard?

   A. 200 ft.

   B. 345 ft.

   C. 450 ft.

   D. 500 ft.

3. What is the actual width of the yard?

   A. 100 ft.

   B. 25 ft.

   C. 150 ft.

   D. 200 ft.

4. What is the actual area of the yard?

   A. 90,000 ft²

   B. 45,000 ft²

   C. 9,000 ft²

   D. 68,000 ft²

5. If the scale factor is more than 1, then the size of the new shape is

   A. Enlarged.

   B. Reduced.

   C. Same.

   D. None of the above.

6. The distance on a map represents 4 cm = 20 meters. What is the scale factor?

   A. 5: 1

   B. 1: 5

   C. 1: 4

   D. 1: 20

7. Vicky has a scale drawing of her bedroom. The scale she used is 1: m. In her drawing, her bedroom is 8 inches long and 12 inches wide. The actual dimensions of her bedroom are 10 feet long and 15 feet long. What is m? (Hint: 1 ft. = 12 in.)

   A. 20

   B. 15

   C. 10

   D. 35

8. If the scale factor is 0.77, then the size of the new shape is

   A. Reduced.

   B. Enlarged.

   C. Same.

   D. None of the above.

The scale drawing of a square window is shown below:

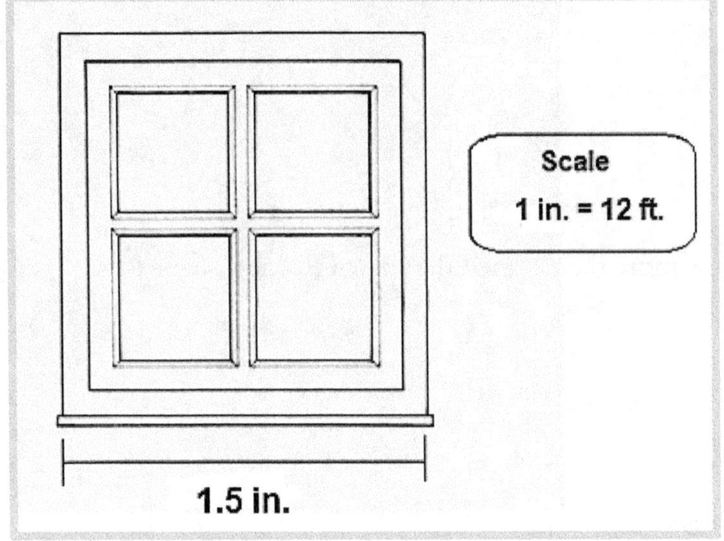

9. What is the perimeter of the actual square window shown in the scale drawing?

   A. 72 in.

   B. 36 ft.

   C. 72 ft.

   D. 48 in.

10. What is the area of the actual square window shown in the scale drawing?

   A. 162 ft^2

   B. 324 ft^2

   C. 324 in^2

   D. 500 in^2

Answer Key:

1) A	6) B
2) C	7) B
3) D	8) A
4) A	9) C
5) A	10) B

Lesson 4: Understand the Pythagorean Theorem and the concepts of congruence and similarity.

The Pythagorean Theorem is a relationship between the sides of a right triangle. In a right triangle, the sides are called the legs and the hypotenuse. The two legs meet at a right angle (90°), and the hypotenuse is the side opposite the right angle.

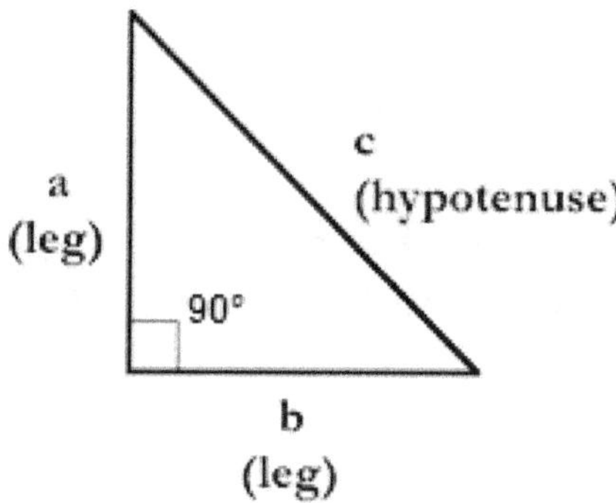

The Pythagorean Theorem states the following:

In a right triangle, the square of the hypotenuse is equal to the sum of the squares of the two legs.

This theorem can be written in one equation:

$$a^2 + b^2 = c^2$$

Congruent Figures

If one shape or geometric figure can become another using rotations, translations, or reflections, then the figures are **congruent**. In other words, congruent figures have the same **shape** and **size**.

Congruent Figures

Similar Figures

Similar figures are the same shape as the real object but not the same size. They maintain the same proportions and angles, but their sizes are different. The **scale factor** is the ratio that compares the side lengths of two similar figures.

Similar figures

Example 1:

The following triangle is a right triangle. Find n.

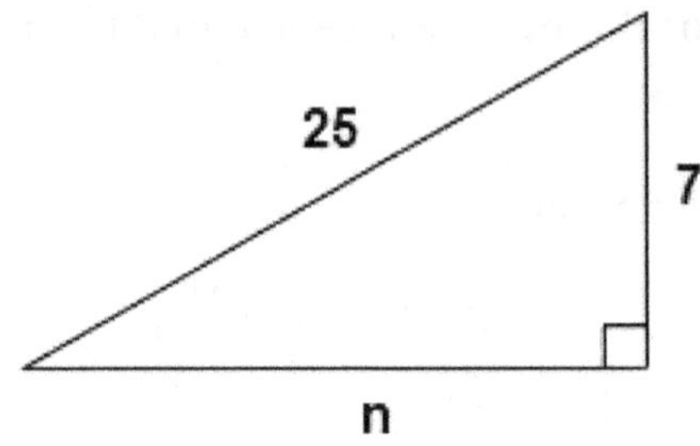

Solution:

Notice that *n* is the leg of the right triangle. Apply the Pythagorean Theorem.

$$a^2 + b^2 = c^2$$

$$n^2 + (7)^2 = (25)^2$$

$$n^2 + 49 = 625$$

Solve the equation.

$$n^2 + 49 = 625$$

$$n^2 = 625 - 49$$

$$n^2 = 576$$

Take the square root of both sides of the equation to eliminate the exponent on the left side.

$$n^2 = 576$$

$$\sqrt{n^2} = \sqrt{576}$$

$$\mathbf{n = 24}$$

Example 2:

The following triangles are similar. What is x?

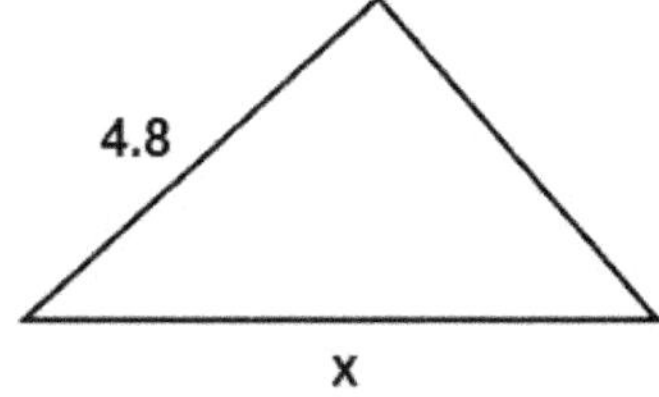
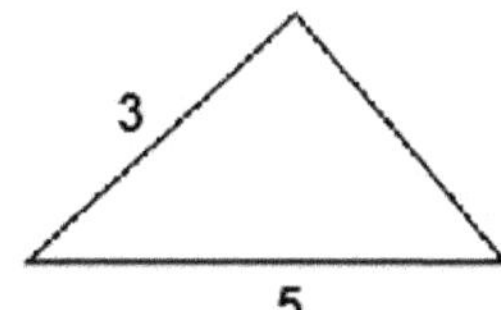

Solution:

Since the triangles are similar, we set up the proportion between the corresponding side lengths.

$$\frac{4.8}{3} = \frac{x}{5}$$

Solve the equation.

$$\frac{4.8}{3} = \frac{x}{5}$$

$$\Rightarrow 3x = (4.8) \cdot (5)$$

$$3x = 24$$

$$x = \frac{24}{3} = \mathbf{8}$$

Practice Exercises

1. The leg of a right triangle is 8 inches and its hypotenuse is 17 inches. What is the measure of its other leg?

   A. 15 in.

   B. 25 in.

   C. 9 in.

   D. 12 in.

2. What is x?

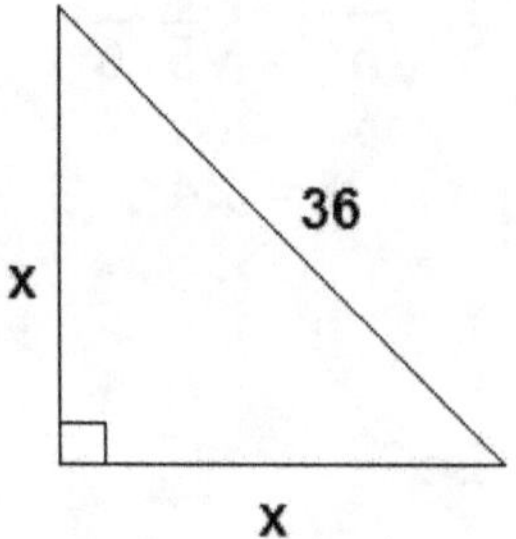

A. 18

B. 12

C. $\sqrt{36}$

D. $\sqrt{18}$

3. Which shape is not congruent to the other three?

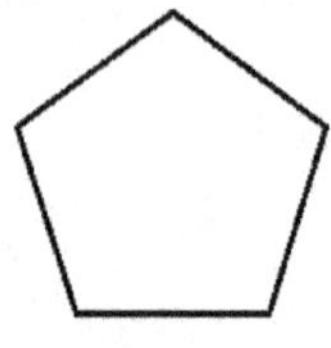

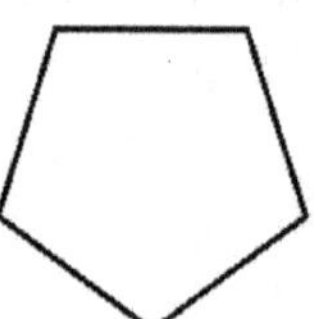

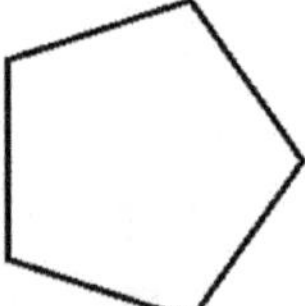

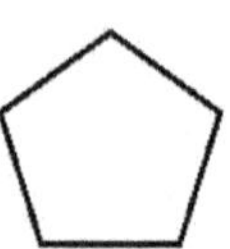

A. Figure A

B. Figure C

C. Figure D

D. Figure B

The following right triangles are similar:

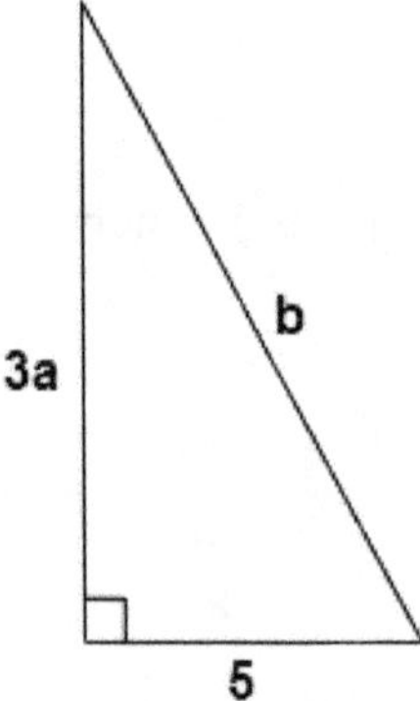

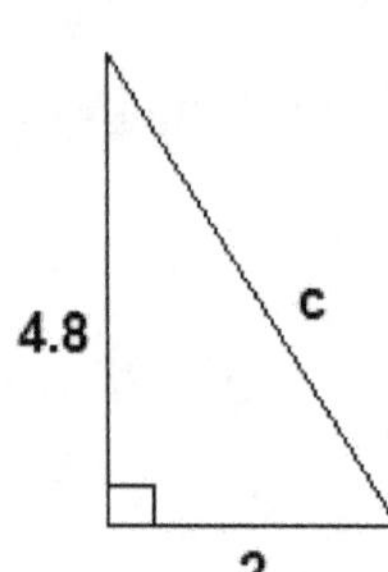

4. What is the value of *a*?

    A. 3

    B. 4

    C. 5

    D. 7

5. What is the value of *b*?

    A. 13

    B. 15

    C. 10

    D. 18

6. What is the value of *c*?

    A. 4.6

    B. 6

    C. 5.2

    D. 3.9

7. What is the scale factor?

    A. 0.6

    B. 0.4

    C. 3.25

    D. 1.5

8. Two legs of a right triangle measure 1 foot and 1 foot. What is the length of the hypotenuse?

    A. $\sqrt{3}$ ft.

    B. 2 ft.

    C. $\sqrt{2}$ ft.

    D. 3 ft.

9. A rectangular field is 55 yards long, and the length of one diagonal of the field is 73 yards. What is the width of the field?

A. 50 yards

B. 48 yards

C. 52 yards

D. 44 yards

10. Two circles, Circle A and Circle B, are congruent to each other. If the radius of Circle A is 10 inches, what is the area of Circle B?

A. 10π in^2.

B. 100π in^2.

C. 20π in^2.

D. 50π in^2.

Answer Key:

1) A		6) C	
2) D		7) B	
3) C		8) C	
4) B		9) B	
5) A		10) B	

REFLECTION ON LEARNING

Answer the following reflection questions and feel free to discuss your responses with your teacher or a classmate.

1- What math ideas and principles did you learn in this chapter?

2- What new math concepts did you learn?

3- What procedures or methods did you practice in this chapter?

4- What aspect of this chapter is still not 100% clear to you?

5- What else do you want your teacher to know?

CHAPTER 5:
DATA ANALYSIS, STATISTICS, AND PROBABILITY

Lesson 1: Understand statistical variability concepts and recognize deviations.

One important aspect of the distribution of data is where its center is located. The **mean,** the **median,** and the **mode** are measures of the center of a data set. They are called **measures of central tendency**.

The **mean** (or average) is the sum of all the values in the set divided by the number of values in the data set. The median is the **middle** number of a sorted list of numbers. The **mode** is the number that appears most frequently in a data set.

The deviations from the pattern occur when certain data points do not fit the overall pattern. For example, a data set can be overall symmetrical except for one value that does not fit the pattern.

Here are two specific deviations:

Outliers: These are data points that are far from other data points. They can be much higher or lower than the rest. The mean is the only measure of central tendency that is always affected by an outlier.

Gaps: Some data sets may have gaps where no data points exist.

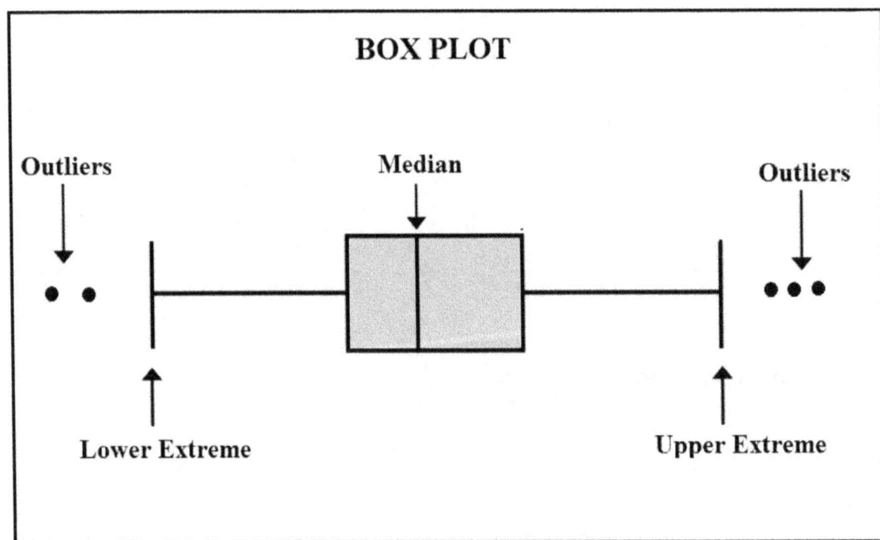

In a symmetrical distribution of data, the mean is the same number as the median and mode.

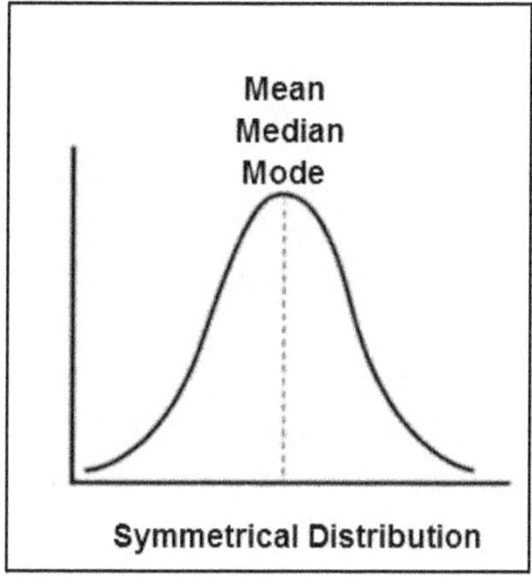

Measures of spread describe how similar or varied the values in a data set are. The simplest way to find the spread in a data set is to identify the **range**, which is the difference between the highest and lowest values in the data set. A larger range indicates a greater spread in the data.

Example:

Find the mean, median, mode, and range of the following set of data: 500, 200, 600, 800, 600, 900, 300, 600, 750, and 650.

Solution:

To calculate the mean, add together all of the numbers in the set and then divide the sum by how many numbers there are. (There are 10 numbers.)

$$\text{Mean} = \frac{500 + 200 + 600 + 800 + 60 + 900 + 300 + 600 + 750 + 650}{10} = \frac{5900}{10} = 590$$

Then, the mean is **590**.

To calculate the median, first place all of the values in numerical order.

200, 300, 500, 600, 600, 600, 650, 750, 800, 900

If we have an odd number of values, the median is the middle number. However, if we have an even number of values, the median will be the mean of the two values in the center of the data set. We have an even number of values, so calculate the mean of the two central values:

200, 300, 500, 600, **600, 600**, 650, 750, 800, 900

$$\text{Mean} = \frac{600 + 600}{2} = \frac{1200}{2} = 600$$

Then, the median is **600**.

The mode is the value that occurs most often. Notice that the value of 600 appears three times. Thus, the mode is **600**.

To calculate the range of the data set, subtract the lowest value from the highest value.

Range = 900 − 200 = **700**

Practice Exercises

1. In a typical set of data, which of the following is true?

    A. The mean is always one of the data values.

    B. The median is always one of the data values.

    C. The mode, if it exists, is always one of the data values.

    D. None of the above.

> The following data set represents the pulse rates (beats per minute)
> of ten students enrolled in a medical test:
> 61, 75, 88, 98, 70, 69, 71, 77, 81, and 90

2. What is the mean pulse?

    A. 80

    B. 78

    C. 76

    D. 75

3. What is the median pulse?

    A. 76

    B. 80

    C. 77

    D. 74

4. What is the mode pulse?

    A. 90

    B. 77

C. 84

D. There is no mode.

5. What is the range of the data set?

   A. 61

   B. 43

   C. 37

   D. 39

6. The following data set represents Kyle's monthly cell phone bill for six months. What is the median phone bill?

$44.56, $58.94, $48.66, $40.17, $53.62, $49.08

   A. $49.08

   B. $48.87

   C. $50.56

   D. $48.66

> The following temperatures were recorded (in degrees Fahrenheit)
> each day for a week:
> 77, 74, 81, 85, 79, 61, 73

7. What is the outlier in the data set, if one exists?

   A. 77

   B. 61

   C. 85

   D. There is no outlier.

8. What is the mean of the data set?

   A. 75.71

   B. 77

   C. 76.50

   D. 78

9. What is the mean for the data set, if the outlier is removed?

    A. 79

    B. 77.56

    C. 80

    D. 78.16

10. The mean for a set of 30 scores is 78. Two more students take the test and their scores are 72 and 64. What is the new mean?

    A. 75.25

    B. 77.38

    C. 76.15

    D. 80.43

Answer Key:

1) C		6) B
2) B		7) B
3) A		8) A
4) D		9) D
5) C		10) B

Lesson 2: Understand and apply the concept of probability.

The probability of a specified event is the chance or likelihood that it will occur. The probability of an event is determined by dividing the number of favorable outcomes by the total number of possible outcomes. This means that probability is **always a number between 0 and 1.**

We can see the mean of probability in the following scale.

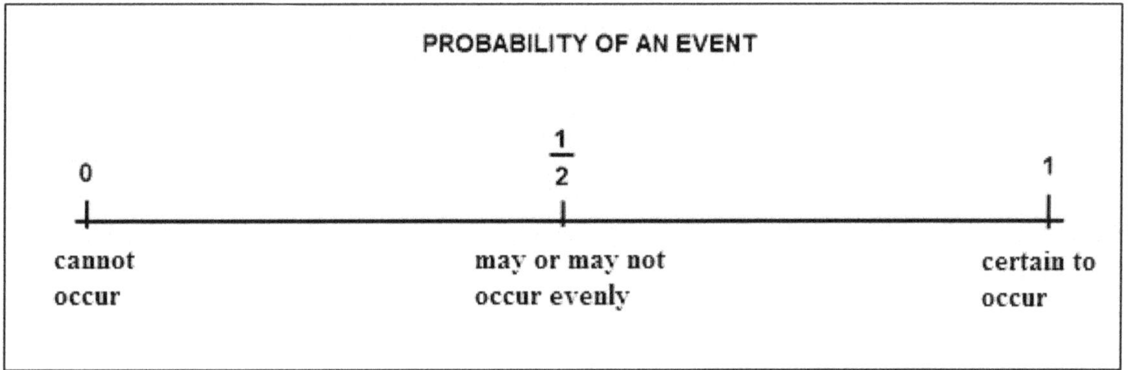

- 0 Probability: The event can never happen because the favorable outcome is zero

- 1 Probability: The event will certainly happen because there is the same number of favorable outcomes as there is total number of outcomes.

- 0.5 Probability: The event has an equal chance of happening or not happening.

- 0 to 0.5 Probability: If an event has a probability between 0 and 0.5, then it is unlikely to happen, but not impossible.

- 0.5 to 1 Probability: If an event has a probability between 0.5 and 1, then it is likely to happen, but not certain.

Probabilities can be expressed in terms of ratios. Since any ratio can be turned into a fraction, decimal, or percent, we can also turn any probability into a **fraction, decimal, or percent.** For example, the probability that a fair coin lands on heads is ½. This probability can be expressed in several forms:

$$P = \frac{1}{2}, \qquad P = 0.5, \qquad P = 50\%$$

Example:

Nick has a bag with 30 cherries, 12 sweet and 18 sour. If he picks a cherry at random, what is the probability that it will be sweet?

Solution:

There are 30 possible cherries that could be picked, so the number of possible outcomes is 30. Of these 30 possible outcomes, 12 are favorable (sweet), so the probability that the cherry will be sweet is:

$$Probability = \frac{Number\ of\ favorable\ outcomes}{Total\ number\ of\ outcomes} = \frac{12}{30} = \frac{2}{5}$$

Thus, the probability that a randomly picked cherry will be sweet is $\frac{2}{5}$ or 0.4 (40%).

Practice Exercises

1. Jason randomly picks a letter from the phrase, "Geometry is easy to learn." What is the probability of choosing a vowel?

   A. 5/21

   B. 3/7

   C. 11/21

   D. 5/7

> A jar contains 8 red marbles numbered 1 to 8, 10 blue marbles numbered 1 to 10, and 6 green marbles numbered 1 to 6. A marble is drawn at random from the jar.

2. What is the probability of choosing a red marble?

   A. 3/4

   B. 2/3

   C. 1/2

   D. 1/3

3. What is the probability of choosing a green marble?

   A. 1/4

   B. 2/5

   C. 1/3

   D. 1/2

4. What is the probability of choosing a marble with the number 5 written on it?

    A. 1/6

    B. 3/5

    C. 1/8

    D. 3/4

5. What is the probability of choosing a blue marble with the number 8 written on it?

    A. 1/24

    B. 5/24

    C. 8/24

    D. 7/24

6. What is the probability of choosing a marble with the number 12 written on it?

    A. 1/2

    B. 1/24

    C. 1

    D. 0

7. Which of the following cannot be a probability of an event?

    A. 6.75%

    B. 0.99

    C. 3/100

    D. 5/2

8. Elizabeth writes each letter of the alphabet on a different slip of paper and puts the slips into a hat. What is the probability of drawing one slip of paper from the hat at random and getting a vowel?

    A. 7/26

    B. 21/26

    C. 5/26

    D. 2/13

9. What is the probability of rolling an odd number on a standard dice?

   A. 25%

   B. 50%

   C. 75%

   D. 80%

10.

What is the probability of choosing a queen from a standard 52 deck of cards?

   A. 1/13

   B. 1/26

   C. 7/52

   D. 7/26

Answer Key:

1) B	6) D
2) D	7) D
3) A	8) C
4) C	9) B
5) A	10) A

Lesson 3: Use 2-way tables to interpret bivariate data.

Two-way tables are a visual representation of the possible relationships between two sets of categorical data. The categories are labeled at the top and the left side of the table, with **the frequency** (count) information appearing in the interior cells of the table.

Two-Way Table

Occupations	Positive Opinion	Negative Opinion	Total
Teachers	45	35	80
Nurses	50	11	61
Total	95	46	141

Example 1:

The following two-way frequency table shows the preference for cats or dogs.

Preference	Lawyers	Doctors
Cats	25	32
Dogs	43	28
No preference	10	15

How many people prefer dogs?

Solution:

Add up the number of lawyers and doctors in the dog's row:

Preference	Lawyers	Doctors
Prefer cats	25	32
Prefer dogs	43	28
No preference	10	15

Then, the number of people that prefer dogs is 43 + 28 = **71**

Practice Exercises

The following two-way table shows a data set about what workers eat for lunch. One categorical variable is job; the other categorical variable is what type of lunch the workers have.

Lunch	Plumbers	Electricians
Pizza	66	47
Hot dog	70	38

1. How many workers prefer pizza?

   A. 113

   B. 136

   C. 66

   D. 120

2. How many workers prefer hot dogs?

   A. 108

   B. 85

   C. 110

   D. 113

3. How many workers were asked?

    A. 198

    B. 230

    C. 219

    D. 221

The following two-way table shows some information about the number of bookcases a factory makes in one year.

	Small	Medium	Large	Total
Pine	235	199	308	
Oak	129	**Y**	413	755
Yew	**X**	181	522	**Z**
Total	665			

4. What is X?

    A. 298

    B. 301

    C. 315

    D. 300

5. What is Y?

    A. 224

    B. 232

    C. 213

    D. 215

6. What is Z?

    A. 1,004

B. 997

C. 1017

D. 999

7. How many bookcases were made in a year?

A. 2,560

B. 1,876

C. 2,501

D. 3,096

The following two-way table shows the preferences for sports in a college.

Sport	Male	Female
Swimming	87	88
Basketball	195	132
Football	**X**	50
Tennis	177	156
Total	702	-

8. What is X?

A. 276

B. 243

C. 245

D. 251

9. How many students were asked?

A. 1,218

B. 1,317

C. 1,130

D. 1,128

10. What percentage of students prefer football?

A. 21.54%

B. 25.97%

C. 32.76%

D. 43.21%

Answer Key:

1) A	6) A
2) A	7) C
3) D	8) B
4) B	9) D
5) C	10) B

REFLECTION ON LEARNING

Answer the following reflection questions and feel free to discuss your responses with your teacher or a classmate.

1- What math ideas and principles did you learn in this chapter?

2- What new math concepts did you learn?

3- What procedures or methods did you practice in this chapter?

4- What aspect of this chapter is still not 100% clear to you?

5- What else do you want your teacher to know?

CHAPTER 6:
PURE MATHEMATICS

Practice Exercises

> Kevin's playlist has four songs:
>
> Song 1 (3.5 minutes)
>
> Song 2 (4 minutes and 30 seconds)
>
> Song 3 (3 minutes and 30 seconds)
>
> Song 4 (5 minutes and 45 seconds)

1. How many minutes does Kevin's playlist last?

2. How many times can Kevin listen to his entire playlist during a 55-minute car ride?

   Emily wants to save 3/8 of her allowance for a trip.

3. What percent of her allowance does she want to save?

4. If her allowance is $230 each month, how much money is she planning to save?

5. Simplify the following expression:

$$\frac{2^{10}}{(4)^3 \cdot \sqrt{4}}$$

6. Write an algebraic expression for the following: *"Twenty added to the product of a number and four is equal to three times the number."* (Use x for the unknown value.)

7. The width of a rectangle is 18 inches, and its perimeter is 80 inches. What is the length of the rectangle?

8. Find the volume of a hemisphere (half of a sphere) with a radius of 10 inches. (Use $\pi = 3.14$)

9. The front row of a theatre has 31 seats. If Paul were asked to occupy the seat at the median position, which seat would Paul occupy?

10. In February, it rained for 12 days. Estimate the probability that it rains on a day in February (Express your answer as a fraction.).

Answer Key:

1) 17.25 minutes

2) 3 times

3) 37.5%

4) $86.25

5) 8

6) $20 + 4x = 3x$

7) 22 inches

8) 2,093.33 cubic inches

9) The 16th seat

10) 3/7

REFLECTION ON LEARNING

Answer the following reflection questions and feel free to discuss your responses with your teacher or a classmate.

1- What math ideas and principles did you learn in this chapter?

2- What new math concepts did you learn?

3- What procedures or methods did you practice in this chapter?

4- What aspect of this chapter is still not 100% clear to you?

5- What else do you want your teacher to know?

> Three teams played the Stock Market Game. They each started out with $18,500 to invest. The winning team is the one with the most money at the end. Team A made 3/4 more money, Team B made 55% more money, and Team C made a total of $31,870.

1. How much money did Team A make?

    A. $13,875

    B. $31,450

    C. $22,790

    D. $32,375

2. How much money did Team B make?

    A. $33,275

    B. $28,675

    C. $10,175

    D. $22,465

3. Which team won the game?

    A. Team B

    B. Team A

    C. Team C

4. Over time, the value of a car decreases. If the value of a car purchased for $24,000 decreased by 12.5% in a year, what would its value be at the end of the year?

    A. $21,000

    B. $19,750

    C. $22,000

    D. $12,500

> Cellular phone service is available for $70 per month for 1,200 minutes.

5. What is the monthly cost in dollars per minute?

    A. $1.71 per minute

    B. $0.583 per minute

    C. $.0.098 per minute

    D. $0.0583 per minute

6. What is the monthly cost in cents per minute?

    A. 58.3 cents per minute

    B. 5.83 cents per minute

    C. 0.58 cents per minute

    D. 6.73 cents per minute

7. How many feet per second are equivalent to 72 miles per hour?

    A. 52.8 feet per second   C. 10.56 feet per second

    B. 108.7 feet per second   D. 105.6 feet per second

8. Simplify the following expression:

$$\left(\frac{7^7 \cdot 7^8}{7^9 \cdot 7^3}\right)^{-1}$$

    A. 1/343   C. 7^{10}

    B. 7^5 D. 343

9. What is the value of x?

50% of x = 0.25x + 20

    A. 40   C. 75

    B. 80   D. 50

Look at the following receipt:

```
              STAPLE-STORE
            LOW PRICES, EVERY DAY
           2344, Staple Furniture Road
           Furniture City, CA, 211232

     SALE                   27981349442287755000
                            10/17/2020    17:23

     QTY        SKU                      PRICE
     1      HAND TOWEL
            023404213519                2.97 N
     4      Office Chair
            069005841315              359.56 N
     1      Office Table
            030424458834              120.89 N
        SUBTOTAL                      $483.42
            Simple Tax   10.25%        $50.27
        TOTAL                            ?

     CREDIT
     Card No .:    xxxxxxxxxxxx 9999
     Chip Read
     Auth No .: 688880
     AID .: 6166TF6V3RC4
```

10. How many items were purchased?

    A. 3   C. 4

    B. 5   D. 6

11. What is the total amount?

    A. $533.69   C. $523.79

    B. $483.42   D. $512.69

12. What is the cost of an office chair?

    A. $359.56   C. $89.89

    B. $91.07   D. $90.75

13. What is the cost of a dozen hand towels?

    A. $14.97   C. $35.64

    B. $23.89   D. $41.23

14. Edward walks 8.75 miles in 3/4 hour. What is the unit rate in miles per hour?

    A. 11.67 miles per hour   C. 12.50 miles per hour

    B. 6.56 miles per hour   D. 3.98 miles per hour

15. Adam can mow a lawn that measures 1, 640 square feet in 3.5 hours. At that rate, how long would it take him to mow a lawn 6, 560 square feet?

    A. 8.5 hours   C. 12.5 hours

    B. 14 hours   D. 10 hours

A bakery charges $4.50 for each cupcake and $5.00 for each brownie. Jessica spent $91.50 purchasing 19 items at the bakery.

16. How many cupcakes did she purchase?

    A. 12   C. 7

    B. 8   D. 5

17. How many brownies did she purchase?

    A. 11   C. 7

    B. 10   D. 12

The population of foxes in a national forest was recorded as 3,450 in 2015 and 5,200 in 2020. Suppose that the population continues to grow linearly.

18. What is the rate of change of this linear model?

    A. 275 foxes per year

    B. 350 foxes per year

    C. 315 foxes per year

    D. 290 foxes per year

19. Which linear function represents the fox population P, in terms of t, the years since 2015?

    A. $P(t) = 420t + 3,450$

    B. $P(t) = 350t + 5,200$

    C. $P(t) = 350t + 3,450$

    D. $P(t) = 210t + 5,200$

20. What is the fox population in 2024?

    A. 6,600

    B. 6,560

    C. 5,870

    D. 7,100

21. When will the population reach 11,500 foxes?

    A. Year 2038

    B. Year 2040

    C. Year 2029

    D. Year 2036

A rectangular tank has a length of 15 feet, a width of 22 feet, and a depth of 6 feet.

22. How many cubic feet of water can the tank hold?

    A. $1,980 \text{ ft}^3$

    B. $2,010 \text{ ft}^3$

    C. 336 ft^3

    D. $1,880 \text{ ft}^3$

23. The manufacturer suggests filling the tank to 85% capacity. How many cubic feet is this?

    A. $1,690 \text{ ft}^3$

    B. $1,715 \text{ ft}^3$

    C. 1695 ft^3

    D. $1,683 \text{ ft}^3$

24. One cubic foot is approximately 7.48 gallons. How many gallons of water should be put in the tank at 85% capacity?

    A. 12,675.46 gal.

    B. 12,588.84 gal.

    C. 13,965.07 gal.

    D. 11,976.44 gal.

25. A box that is 18 inches wide, 30 inches high, and 4 inches thick is to be wrapped in gift paper. How many square inches of gift paper are needed?

A. 2,160 in^2

B. 1,520 in^2

C. 1,388 in^2

D. 1,464 in^2

26. A map scale indicates that 2/5 inches on the map corresponds with 4 real miles. How many miles apart are two cities that are 3.5 inches apart on the map?

A. 27 miles

B. 32 miles

C. 35 miles

D. 30 miles

27. A tree that is 33 feet tall casts a shadow 16 feet long. Brittany is 6 feet tall. How long is Brittany's shadow? (Hint: use similar triangles.)

A. 3.2 ft.

B. 4.3 ft.

C. 2.9 ft.

D. 8.8 ft.

28. Michael runs 7 miles north and 8 miles east. What is the shortest distance he must travel to return to his starting point?

A. 15 miles

B. $\sqrt{15}$ miles

C. 11.3 miles

D. $\sqrt{113}$ miles

29. What is x?

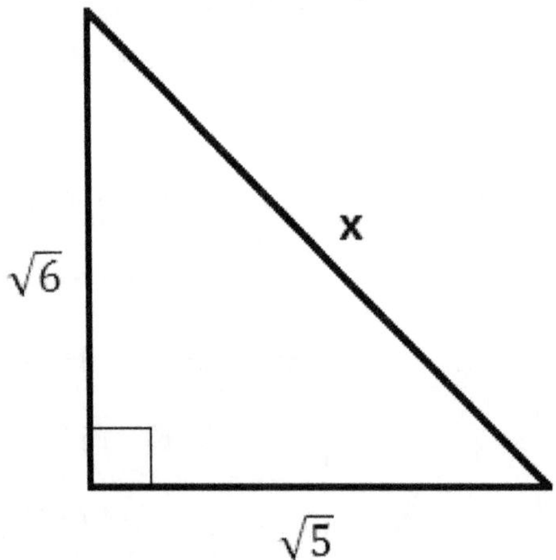

A. 11

B. $\sqrt{11}$

C. $\sqrt{6} + \sqrt{5}$

D. 12

The following table shows the number of survey subjects who received speeding tickets in the last year and those who did not, categorized by the colors of their cars.

Color of Car	Speeding Ticket	No Speeding Ticket	Total
Black car	24	156	A
Blue car	63	357	B
Total	87	513	600

30. What is the value of A?

    A. 340

    B. 180

    C. 200

    D. 170

31. What is the value of B?

    A. 400

    B. 385

    C. 420

    D. 410

32. What is the probability that a randomly chosen person has a black car?

    A. 0.30

    B. 0.25

    C. 0.42

    D. 0.77

33. What is the probability that a randomly chosen person has a blue car?

    A. 0.35

    B. 0.65

    C. 0.82

    D. 0.70

34. What is the probability that a randomly chosen person has a black car **and** got a speeding ticket?

    A. 0.40

    B. 0.04

    C. 0.10

    D. 0.14

35. The mean of the following data set is 23.2. What is x?

22, 31, x, 16, 29

A. 18

B. 43

C. 15

D. 19

36. A professor has recorded test grades for 20 students in his class, but one of the grades is no longer readable. If the mean score on the test was 85 and the mean of the 19 readable scores is 91, what is the value of the unreadable score?

A. 57

B. 71

C. 29

D. 35

REFLECTION ON LEARNING

Answer the following reflection questions and discuss your responses with your teacher or a classmate.

1- How do you feel about your performance on the test?

2- Which types of questions were difficult for you?

3- How do you feel about your time management strategies?

4- What specific things do you want to do differently next time? List them.

5- What math functions or content areas do you want to review? List them.

6- What else do you want your teacher to know?

1) D	13) C	25) D
2) B	14) A	26) C
3) B	15) B	27) C
4) A	16) C	28) D
5) D	17) D	29) B
6) B	18) B	30) B
7) D	19) C	31) C
8) A	20) A	32) A
9) B	21) A	33) D
10) D	22) A	34) B
11) A	23) D	35) A
12) C	24) B	36) C

1. Rose watched a turtle crawl 4.70 feet in one hour. The next hour, the turtle crawled 33/5 feet. How far did the turtle crawl in total?

   A. 37.5 ft.   C. 12.6 ft.

   B. 11.3 ft.   D. 9.9 ft.

2. Luke skated for 18.5 hours last week. This week, he skated 30% more. How long did he skate this week?

   A. 5.55 hours   C. 24.05 hours

   B. 23.75 hours   D. 25 hours

3. Out of 520 racers who started a marathon, 485 completed the race, 30 gave up, and 5 were disqualified. What percentage did not complete the marathon?

   A. 5.77%   C. 7.45%

   B. 6.08%   D. 6.73%

4. Megan ran 1,650 meters in 6 minutes and 45 seconds. What is the unit rate in meters per second?

   A. 4.07 meters per second   C. 247.8 meters per second

   B. 6.75 meters per second   D. 260 meters per second

5. A car is going at 90 miles per hour. How far does it travel in 50 seconds?

   A. 12.5 miles   C. 1.25 miles

   B. 7.5 miles   D. 2.25 miles

6. 35 % of 2x is equal to 24.5. What is x?

   A. 70   C. 39

   B. 48   D. 35

7. Compute the following:

$$\frac{\sqrt{1} + \sqrt{100} + \sqrt{625}}{\sqrt[3]{8}}$$

   A. 18   C. 9

   B. 36   D. 12

8. Simplify the following expression:

$$\frac{(10^3 \cdot 100^2)^2}{(10^5)^0}$$

A. 100

C. 10^{10}

B. 10^9

D. 10^{14}

Look at the following gas station receipt:

```
Passmore Gas & Propane
FG62326873455
3685 Charles Street
Livonia, MT
81065


9/12/2018   576646188
11:54 AM

XXXXXXXXXXXX2323
visa
INVOICE 831332
AUTH 138864

PUMP#24
Regular                 19.58G
PRICE/GAL               $2.98

FUEL TOTAL                .?

                   ----------
   Total =                 ?
CREDIT
=============================
```

9. What is the price of a gallon of gas?

   A. $3.15

   C. $19.58

   B. $2.98

   D. $6.57

10. What is the total amount?

   A. $56.66

   C. $58.35

   B. $58.74

   D. $60.12

11. What is the cost of 25 gallons of gas?

   A. $75.00

   C. $74.50

   B. $76.50

   D. $78.99

12. Katy walks 6.20 miles in 1.25 hours. What is the unit rate in miles per hour?

   A. 4.88 miles per hour

   B. 5.17 miles per hour

   C. 4.53 miles per hour

   D. 4.96 miles per hour

13. A firefighter truck can hold 4,200 gallons of water. A firefighter can deliver 210 gallons of water every three minutes. How long will it take for the firefighter to empty the tank?

   A. 53 minutes and 20 seconds

   B. 60 minutes

   C. 52 minutes and 50 seconds

   D. 70 minutes

14. Solve the following pair of simultaneous linear equations:

$$M + N = 480$$

$$M - N = 88$$

   A. $M = 284, N = 196$

   B. $M = 196, N = 284$

   C. $M = 296, N = 184$

   D. $M = 266, N = 214$

15. Susan wrote the following algebraic expression: **6x − 0.75x**. What would be the phrase that represents the algebraic expression?

   A. Six minus the product of 0.75 and a number

   B. Six times a number minus 0.75

   C. The difference between six times a number and 75% of the number

   D. The difference between six times a number and 0.75

> A company sells smartphones. They incur a fixed cost of $15,500 for rent, insurance, and other expenses. It costs $58 to produce each smartphone. Let x be the number of smartphones produced.

16. What is the linear function that represents the cost C of the company as a function of x?

   A. $C(x) = 58 + 15{,}500x$

   B. $C(x) = 15{,}500 + 58x$

   C. $C(x) = 15{,}500 - 58x$

   D. $C(x) = 58 - 15{,}500x$

17. What is the cost of producing 1,000 smartphones?

   A. $68,500

   B. $80,000

   C. $72,000

   D. $73,500

18. If the company does not produce a single smartphone, what is the total cost?

   A. $15,542
   B. $15,500
   C. $15,000
   D. $15,558

19. To complete a job, five workers get paid at the rate of $18.50 per hour. If the total payment for the job was $647.50, how many hours did the five workers spend on the job?

   A. 7 hours
   B. 8.5 hours
   C. 6 hours
   D. 9.5 hours

20. Which shape has the most corners?

   A. Cuboid
   B. Hexagon
   C. Equilateral triangle
   D. Trapezoid

21. Which of the following is true?

   A. The volume of a square is more than 1.
   B. The surface area of a pyramid is measured in cubic inches.
   C. The hemisphere has no corners.
   D. Congruent figures have different sizes.

22. The surface area of a cube is 0.54 square feet. What is the volume of the cube?

   A. 0.027 ft^3
   B. 0.27 ft^3
   C. 2.70 ft^3
   D. 27 ft^3

23. A cylinder with a base radius of 10 inches and a height of 14 inches is to be wrapped in gift paper. How many square inches of gift paper are needed? (use $\pi = 3.14$)

   A. $4,396 \text{ in}^2$
   B. $1,504.8 \text{ in}^2$
   C. $2,198 \text{ in}^2$
   D. $1,510.8 \text{ in}^2$

24. A map scale indicates that x inches on the map correspond with 5 real miles. Two towns that are 7.5 inches apart on the map represent 100 real miles. What is x?

   A. 0.525
   B. 0.800
   C. 0.375
   D. 0.405

25. If the scale factor is 8/9, then the size of the new shape is

   A. The same.
   B. Enlarged.
   C. Reduced.
   D. None of the above.

26. Lori drives 12 miles south and 35 miles west. What is the shortest distance she must travel to return to this starting point?

A. 37 miles

B. $\sqrt{47}$ miles

C. 43 miles

D. $\sqrt{23}$ miles

27. What is x?

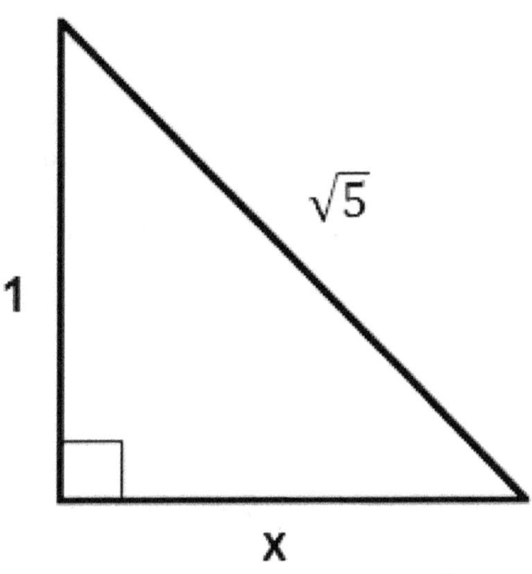

A. 4

B. $\sqrt{3}$

C. $\sqrt{2}$

D. 2

Home pregnancy tests were given to a group of women. The following table shows the home pregnancy test results:

Pregnancy Status	Positive Test	Negative Test	Total
Pregnant	67	8	75
Not Pregnant	A	23	C
Total	78	B	109

28. What is the value of A?

A. 11

B. 13

C. 21

D. 10

29. What is the value of B?

A. 29

B. 34

C. 31

D. 30

30. What is the value of C?

A. 37

B. 34

C. 29

D. 30

31. What is the probability that a woman from the group is not pregnant?

A. 21.10%

B. 27.85%

C. 31.19%

D. 30.06%

32. What is the probability that a woman from the group got a positive test?

A. 61.47%

B. 70.23%

C. 68.97%

D. 71.56%

33. The mean of the following data set is 174.5. What is x?

$$160, 170, 172, 172, 175, x, 182, 185$$

A. 180

B. 176

C. 188

D. 178

> The following data set shows scores on a math test:
> 94, 27, 81, 77, 85, 79, 70, 84, 91

34. What is the mean of the data set?

A. 80

B. 76.4

C. 81.1

D. 77

35. What is the median of the data set?

A. 85

B. 81

C. 79

D. 8

36. What is the outlier in the data set, if one exists?

A. 27

B. 94

C. 91

D. There is no outlier.

REFLECTION ON LEARNING

Answer the following reflection questions and discuss your responses with your teacher or a classmate.

1- How do you feel about your performance on the test?

2- Which types of questions were difficult for you?

3- How do you feel about your time management strategies?

4- What specific things do you want to do differently next time? List them.

5- What math functions or content areas do you want to review? List them.

6- What else do you want your teacher to know?

1) B	13) B	25) C
2) C	14) A	26) A
3) D	15) C	27) D
4) A	16) B	28) A
5) C	17) D	29) C
6) D	18) B	30) B
7) A	19) A	31) C
8) D	20) A	32) D
9) B	21) C	33) A
10) C	22) A	34) B
11) C	23) B	35) B
12) D	24) C	36) A

About CBL

At CBL, we promote systematic solutions, learner-centered textbooks, and forward-thinking strategies in adult education, workforce development, and vocational training. Our diverse solutions and products are intricately designed to enrich students' learning experiences while making the job of busy, hard-working adult instructors easier.

CBL takes pride in publishing student-centered textbooks designed to prepare learners for CASAS, TABE 11&12, HiSET, and GED assessments and assist instructors in covering course curricula and standards with confidence.

Our publications also include teaching guides, test prep tools, and study guides that foster reflective learning, ensuring sustained engagement in active learning. Find our meticulously crafted textbooks on our book page (cbledu.com) or major platforms like Amazon, Barnes & Noble, and Ingram Spark.

CBL also guides adult education and workforce programs in establishing robust professional development programs—training, peer-mentoring, coaching, community of practices (CoPs), and instructional systems— fostering a culture of continuous improvement and contributing to higher learner retention and success rates. We also offer workshops and PD sessions for adult educators and classroom instructors.

If you have questions about instructional systems, textbooks, or student learning and retention, contact us today at teamcbl@cbledu.com or 410-960-4082.

MORE TEXTBOOKS BY CBL

ADULT ED
MATH
NUMBER SYSTEM, NUMBER SENSE, AND OPERATIONS PREPARING
FOR
CASAS, TABE 11 & 12, HISET, AND GED TESTING
BY COACHING FOR BETTER LEARNING

ADULT ED
MATH
GEOMETRY PREPARING
FOR
CASAS, TABE 11 & 12, HISET, AND GED TESTING
BY COACHING FOR BETTER LEARNING

CBL COACHING
Math
Practice Worksheets and Workbook for Adult Students
A learner-centered tool designed to help students practice and master the four operations while preparing them for CASAS Math GOALS 2, TABE 11 and 12, ACT, HiSET, GED tests, and IET programs.

SKILLS FOR SUCCESS IN CAREER AND TECHNICAL EDUCATION (CTE)
STUDENT GUIDE
A SYSTEMATIC WAY TO MASTER ORGANIZATIONAL AND SOFT SKILLS
CBL COACHING

HOW TO ACHIEVE BETTER STUDENT RETENTION IN ADULT EDUCATION
Secrets to becoming an indispensable adult-ed teacher that provides a learning experience that's hard to walk away from (and keeps administrators happy)
TEDDY EDOUARD

TABE 11 & 12 CONSUMABLE STUDENT READING MANUAL FOR LEVEL E
Preparing Adult Learners for TABE 11 & 12 Reading Tests and for Vocational Training and College Entrance Reading Exams
By Coaching for Better Learning, LLC

TABE 11 & 12 CONSUMABLE STUDENT READING MANUAL FOR LEVEL M
Preparing Adult Learners for TABE 11 & 12 Reading Tests and for Vocational Training and College Entrance Reading Exams
By Coaching for Better Learning, LLC

TABE 11 & 12 CONSUMABLE STUDENT READING MANUAL FOR LEVEL D
Preparing Adult Learners for TABE 11 & 12 Reading Tests and for Vocational Training and College Entrance Reading Exams
By Coaching for Better Learning, LLC

TABE 11 & 12 STUDENT LANGUAGE MANUAL FOR LEVEL E
Preparing Adult Learners for TABE 11 & 12 Language Tests and for Vocational Training and College Entrance Exams
By Coaching for Better Learning, LLC

TABE 11 & 12 STUDENT LANGUAGE MANUAL FOR LEVEL M
Preparing Adult Learners for TABE 11 & 12 Language Tests and for Vocational Training and College Entrance Exams
By Coaching for Better Learning, LLC

TABE 11 & 12 Consumable Student Math Workbook FOR LEVEL E
Preparing Adult Learners for TABE 11 & 12 Math Tests and for Vocational Training Entrance Math Exams
By Coaching for Better Learning, LLC

TABE 11 & 12 Consumable Student Math Workbook FOR LEVEL M
Preparing Adult Learners for TABE 11 & 12 Math Tests and for Vocational Training Entrance Math Exams
By Coaching for Better Learning, LLC

TABE 11 & 12 Consumable Student Math Workbook FOR LEVEL D
Preparing Adult Learners for TABE 11 & 12 Math Tests and for Vocational Training Entrance Math Exams
By Coaching for Better Learning, LLC

TABE 11 & 12 Consumable Student Math Workbook FOR LEVEL A
Preparing Adult Learners for TABE 11 & 12 Math Tests and for Vocational Training Entrance Math Exams
By Coaching for Better Learning, LLC

CBL COACHING
Workbook
Number and Letter Tracing for Adult Students
This tool is designed to help adult students practice and master handwriting. It is appropriate for literacy, ESL, and ABE classes.

READING NOTEBOOK & JOURNAL
For Adult Students
By Coaching For Better Learning CBL COACHING

MATH NOTEBOOK & JOURNAL
For Adult Students
By Coaching For Better Learning CBL COACHING

BOOK 1
PHONICS AND LIFE SKILLS READING FOR Adult Literacy, ABE, and ESL Students
Turning Learners into Proficient Readers
CBL COACHING

BOOK 2
PHONICS AND LIFE SKILLS READING FOR Adult Literacy, ABE, and ESL Students
Turning Learners into Proficient Readers
CBL COACHING

BOOK 3
PHONICS AND LIFE SKILLS READING FOR Adult Literacy, ABE, and ESL Students
Turning Learners into Proficient Readers
CBL COACHING

www.ingramcontent.com/pod-product-compliance
Lightning Source LLC
Chambersburg PA
CBHW081945160726
47999CB00008B/2517

9 798330 388547